SAMUEL BECKETT
A Critical Study

SAMUEL BECKETT

A Critical Study

New Edition, with a Supplementary Chapter

By Hugh Kenner

UNIVERSITY OF CALIFORNIA PRESS

Berkeley and Los Angeles   1968

This book is for
VIVIAN MERCIER,
polymath.

Contents

Preface

> But you must know something, said Mr. Hackett.
> One does not part with five shillings to a shadow.
> Nationality, family, birthplace, confession, occupa-
> tion, means of existence, distinctive signs, you can-
> not be in ignorance of all this.
> Utter ignorance, said Mr. Nixon.
>
> — *Watt*

This book, meant not to explain Samuel Beckett's
work but to help the reader think about it, bears such
evidence of Mr. Beckett's courtesy that I must caution the
reader against mistaking it for an authorized exposition.
That sort of misunderstanding will proliferate for decades, as anyone knows who has traced the course of the
Joyce legend. Let me therefore, though the book could
not have been written without its subject's assistance,
put on record the exact extent of his contribution to it.
He placed at my disposal three jettisoned typescripts:
Mercier et Camier, Eleutheria, and "Premier Amour";
he answered such questions of fact and date as I thought
it worth while to trouble him with; and during a conversation in the spring of 1958 he made various remarks
which sometimes confirmed my hunches, sometimes cor-
rected them, and sometimes suggested lines of thought
on which I should not otherwise have stumbled.

He denied, for instance, the presence in his work of
some hidden plan or key like the parallels in *Ulysses.*
Joyce, he recalled, used to claim that every syllable in
the Joycean canon could be justified, but while that was

one way to write it was not the only way. He then suggested that overinterpretation, which appeared to trouble him more than erroneous interpretation, arose from two main assumptions: that the writer is necessarily presenting some experience which he has had, and that he necessarily writes in order to affirm some general truth (this knocks out most of the theories about *Godot*). He stated that he knew very little about the race of literary beings he called "my people"; no more, in fact, than appears in the books; this led to an anecdote about an actor who in despair threw over the part of Pozzo when the author was unable to enlighten him on a dozen points concerning the character's age, race, occupation, social status, education, philosophy of life. It was clear from the drift of his talk that if Godot, for instance, really crosses the stage under a pseudonym, or if Moran actually becomes Molloy, these events (to say the least) happen without the author's knowledge; nor is Miss Fitt, as has been conjectured, in the author's private mind the Dark Lady of the Sonnets.

We are not, in short, like dogs excited by the scent of invisible meat, to snap after some item of information which the author grasps very well and is holding just behind the curtain. So to proceed is to misapprehend the quality of the Beckett universe, which is permeated by mystery and bounded by a darkness; to assail those qualities because they embarrass the critic's professional knowingness is cheap, reductive, and perverse. Like primitive astronomers, we are free to note recurrences, cherish symmetries, and seek if we can means of placating the hidden powers: more for our comfort than for theirs.

I hope the reader finds these revelations too elementary to require stating; but since they are endorsed by a man who has been familiar with the Beckett universe longer than the reader has, or thari I have, it seems worth while to write them out.

I ask him to believe, then, that Mr. Beckett exists, that he is capable of discussing what he has written, and that he said on a certain occasion approximately the things I have just set down, or things very like them. I also ask him to believe (for there were no human witnesses) that on leaving Mr. Beckett's apartment I became confused in the courtyard, and applying myself to the wrong door, instead of the street I blundered into a cul-de-sac which contained two ash cans and a bicycle.

1961

Six years later I abstain from afterthoughts, and change only printer's errors. A supplementary chapter says what I have to say about his recent work. Though for English readers *Comment C'est* has since become *How It Is,* I have let the French title stand, and the translated excerpts, blander than the ones available now. Beckett made them, finding my own attempts "groggy," and they merit preserving as transitional stages between a stark French book and its equally stark English sibling.

1967

The Man in the Room

Who knows what the ostrich sees in the sand?
— *Murphy*

1

Mr. Beckett's patient concern with bicycles, amputees, battered hats, and the letter M; his connoisseurship of the immobilized hero; his preoccupation with footling questions which there isn't sufficient evidence to resolve; his humor of the short sentence; his Houdini-like virtuosity (by preference chained hand and foot, deprived of story, dialogue, locale) : these constitute a unique comic repertoire, like a European clown's. The antecedents of his plays are not in literature but—to take a rare American example—in Emmett Kelly's solemn determination to sweep a circle of light into a dustpan: a haunted man whose fidelity to an impossible task—quite as if someone he desires to oblige had exacted it of him—illuminates the dynamics of a tragic sense of duty. ("We are waiting for Godot to come—Or for night to fall. We have kept our appointment and that's an end to that. We are not saints, but we have kept our appointment. How many people can boast as much?") The milieu of his novels bears a moral resemblance to that of the circus, where virtuosity —to no end—is the principle of life, where a thousand variations on three simple movements fill up the time between train and train, and the animals have merely to pace their cages to draw cries of admiring sympathy that are withheld, whatever his risks, from the high-wire acrobat: the spectators settled numbly in their ritual of waiting, the normal emotions of human solidarity not perverted but anesthetized.

Anesthetized, as at a rite: an execution, for instance. The clown's routine is a pantomime dialogue with his executioners, who paid for their tickets in that universe to which he has no access, outside the tent. So Mr. Beckett's Unnamable, in a place

> which is merely perhaps the inside of my distant skull where once I wandered, now am fixed, lost for tininess, or straining against the walls, with my head, my hands, my feet, my back, and ever murmuring my old stories, my old story, as if it were the first time,

cringes from unspecified Others:

> Perhaps they are watching me from afar, I have no objection, as long as I don't see them, watching me like a face in the embers which they know is doomed to crumble, but it takes too long, it's getting late, eyes are heavy and tomorrow they must rise betimes. So it is I who speak, all alone, since I can't do otherwise.

This clown, a sort of 4 A.M. Pagliacci, is an extreme case, his language an anxious audible dumb show, in a work from which Beckett has succeeded in abolishing all content save the gestures of the intellect: immaculate solipsism compelled (this is the comic twist) to talk, talk, talk, and fertile in despairing explanations of its own garrulity ("It is all very well to keep silence, but one has also to consider the kind of silence one keeps."). Another of his personae, a tattered outcast in the classic clown's outfit—clothes too long and too tight, bowler hat, pants supported by a necktie—manifests a finer self-sufficiency. He is leaning against a wall plying his trade ("I shifted my weight from one foot to the other, and my hands clutched the lapels of my greatcoat. To beg with your hands in your pockets makes a bad impression.") when an orator assails him:

> Look at this down and out, he vociferated, this leftover. If he doesn't go down on all fours, it's for fear of being impounded. . . . Every day you pass them by, resumed the orator, and when you have backed a winner you fling them a farthing. Do you ever think? The voice, Certainly not. A penny, resumed the orator, tuppence—. The voice, Thruppence. It nevers enters your head, resumed the orator, that your charity is a crime, an incentive to slavery, stultification and organized murder. Take a good look at this living corpse. . . . Then he bent forward and took me to task. I had perfected my board. It now consisted of two boards hinged together, which enabled me, when my work was done, to fold it and carry it under my arm. I like to do little odd jobs. So I took off the rag, pocketed the few coins I had earned, untied the board, folded it and put it under my arm. Do you hear me you crucified bastard! cried the orator. Then I went away, although it was still light.

Impervious to the most perfervid artillery of social protest, this man's fine rhetoric of indifference (preoccupied with the technology of begging) illustrates Beckett's invincibly comic method, which locates comedy in the very movements of the human mind. The human mind, viewed from his specialized angle, can even find a use for the *Times Literary Supplement*:

> And in winter, under my greatcoat, I wrapped myself in swathes of newspaper, and did not shed them until the earth awoke, for good, in April. The Times Literary Supplement was admirably adapted to this purpose, of neverfailing toughness and impermeability. Even farts made no impression on it.

And the bum who is determined to exact nourishment

from a stray cow ("She dragged me across the floor, stopping from time to time only to kick me. . . . Clutching the dug with one hand, I kept my hat under it with the other.") is funnier in his determination than in his posture. ("I reproached myself," he continues, "I could no longer count on this cow and she would warn the others. More master of myself I might have made a friend of her. She would have come every day, perhaps accompanied by other cows. I might have learned to make butter, even cheese. But I said to myself, No, all is for the best.")

The central Beckett situations are outrageously simple: a man named Malone, for instance, is in bed, presumably in a sort of poorhouse, dying. And the Beckett comedy lies so far from word play that it can pass intact from language to language: the trilogy of novels, *Molloy, Malone Meurt, L'Innommable,* was written in French about 1948, and the English translations, mostly the author's own, are very close. The comedy he has made his province brings something new to the resources of literature. It is prior to action and more fundamental than language: the process of the brain struggling with ideas ("It's human, a lobster couldn't do it.") : precisely the process (he will no doubt not mind us noting) that has landed western civilization in its present fix.

Malone, for instance, cannot simply lie still and die. He must make up stories, and the hero of his story must roll over on the ground and lose his hat (for these are realistic stories: a careless yarn spinner would have forgotten the hat), and Malone must speculate on the way of this: "For when, lying on your stomach in a wild and practically illimitable part of the country, you turn over on your back, then there is a sideways movement of the whole body, including the head, unless you make a point of avoiding it, and the head comes to rest x inches approximately from where it was before, x being the width of the shoulders in inches, for the head is right in the middle of the shoulders." Not otherwise did Newton take stock of falling apples. A moment later he is noting that one tends less to clutch the ground when on one's back than when on one's stomach: "There is a curious remark which might be worth following up."

Malone in bed bears curious analogies with Descartes, whose speculations, notoriously detached from the immediate inspection of visible and audible things, were by preference pursued in the same place. Descartes has at some time fixed a good deal of Mr. Beckett's attention. The marks of this are perfectly clear in *The Unnamable,* the protagonist of which knows that he thinks but would like to feel certain that he exists, as well as in *Molloy,* where the body (at first hardly distinguishable from a bicycle) is as clearly a machine as Descartes established it was, though here a machine subject to loss and decay. This Cartesian focus is something more than a pedantic coincidence. The philosophy which has stood behind all subsequent philosophies, and which makes the whole of intelligible reality depend on the mental processes of a solitary man, came into being at about the same time as the curious literary form called the novel, which has since infected all other literary genres. The novel, for all its look of objectivity, is the product of an arduous solitary ordeal: you can sing your poems and arrange to have your plays acted, but all you can do with your novels is write them, alone in a room, assembling what memories you can of experiences you had before your siege in the room commenced, all the time secretly perhaps a little ashamed of the genre you are practicing. How can all these lies be taken seriously, and all this local color? Joyce sought to put in everything, once and for all, and be done with it.

2

An answer, or one part of one answer, is that Malone making up stories is free within his own mind, and enjoying the only freedom toward which Beckett's clowns aspire. The outward sign of this freedom is apt to be confused by hasty readers, not to mention the police, with total collapse. Have we not the obligation to set an example of industry? Yet every Beckett tramp is convinced in his heart that inner peace is ideally timeless, enclosed in a parenthesis ideally as long as life.

Early in his career, when he was reading Italian at Trinity College, Beckett discovered in the fourth Canto of the *Purgatorio* one of his most persistent prototypes, the Florentine Belacqua who has a whole lifetime to recline in the shade of a rock. This is not the official way of putting it. The books of Heaven regard this long indolence on the low slopes of Purgatory as a sentence Belacqua is serving because he repented late. He must stay there until the heavens have revolved as often as they did in his life. But waiting, clearly, has always been to his taste, for Dante smiles recalling the legendary torpitude of his old friend back in Florence. "Sedendo et quiescendo anima efficitur sapiens," he used to quote when Dante upbraided him, and now his "Brother, what avails it to ascend?" falls on the ears of the purposeful Dante with a double meaning. By the terms of his sentence it would indeed be useless for him to challenge the angelic majordomo just yet, unless someone's prayer should shorten his term; but it is doubtful if he would welcome a prayer's interference with this opportunity of dreaming over, at his ease, a whole life spent in dreaming.

(*Sedendo et quiescendo* . . . this is a gloss on the turbulent grotesques, Cooper in *Murphy* and Clov in *Endgame*, whom a physical abnormality—we are given its scientific name, acathisia—prevents from sitting.)

Belacqua dreaming of Belacqua dreaming—the life in the mind repeating the life "from the spermarium to the crematorium"—holds such powerful appeal for Murphy that he actually hopes he may live to be old, the longer to serve so blissful a post-mortem sentence. "God grant no godly chandler would shorten his time with a good prayer." The image has great appeal for Murphy's author also, containing neatly as it does the situation of an author who spends working time among remembered landscapes. The Beckett country, name it or leave it nameless as he will, lies always south of Dublin, around his home suburb of Foxrock (which above the train time melee in *All That Fall* we can barely hear the stationmaster announcing as "Boghill.") It is to the station near the Leopardstown racecourse that Mrs. Rooney toils, encountering on her way the Clerk of the Course; here, too, we may locate Watt's descent from the train out of Dublin to commence his sojourn with the remotely paternal Mr. Knott. Two miles away is the institution conducted by the Hospitaller Brothers of St. John of God, where Macmann takes refuge ("You are now in the House of Saint John of God, with the number one hundred and sixty-six. Fear nothing.") . Bally, hub of the Molloy country, is undoubtedly Baile atha Cliath itself, and Malone in bed reliving the nights when he lay in bed as a boy listening to the barking of dogs from the hovels up in the hills where the stonecutters lived, is himself a reliving of a boy who lay listening at night to such sounds from the hills west of Carrickmines, the Belacqua dream within a dream here carried to three terms, and yielding Beckett one of his most hauntingly evocative passages:

> Then in my bed, in the dark, on stormy nights, I could tell from one another, in the outcry without, the leaves, the boughs, the groaning trunks, even the grasses and the house that sheltered me. Each tree had its own cry, just as no two whispered alike, when the air was still. . . .

A page later Malone returns to his fiction about Sapo/Macmann, and notes with some surprise, "And yet I write about myself with the same pencil, and in the same exercise-book as about him." And for that sentence too, on Malone's behalf, Beckett held the pen (or pencil).

It is a kind of memory, yet not memory, this shadowy portentous landscape where identities are so in question, like the ball Dan Rooney dropped which looks like a kind of ball and yet is not a ball.

> MR. ROONEY: Give it to me.
> MRS. ROONEY: (*giving it*) What *is* it, Dan?
> MR. ROONEY: It is a thing I carry about with me.
> MRS. ROONEY: Yes, but what—
> MR. ROONEY: (*violently*) It is a thing I carry about with me!

3

In the novelist's workroom, as he watches the hand with the pen scribble its way free from the shadow of his head and then leap back, these things he carries about absorb his attention.

Beckett's principal siege in the room commenced about 1945, in ravaged France, and lasted until 1950. On that prolonged séance his fame rests: *Godot* and the trilogy were its issue. The bleak stare in the photographs which determine the public image of Samuel Beckett suggests the assault of our daylight, after six years, on a countenance long immured. That face is not strained by the ordeal of conception, but haunted by the memory of having conceived. No other writing so steeps us in total aversion from whatever the present immediacy may be: absorption, possession, by a time and place cloudily remembered, elsewhere, nowhere. The achievement dignifies Peggy Guggenheim's account of the diffident young man of about thirty whom she called Oblomov because he spent most of his days in bed: that was, it now appears, apprenticeship or Cartesian preparation for the creative ordeal that commenced in 1945, in the author's fortieth year.

He was then just back from a first gloomy inspection of postwar Ireland, where his mother lived. Postwar Ireland he found no more fit to sustain consciousness than the Ireland he had been visiting the month the war broke out. ("I immediately returned to France. I preferred France in war to Ireland in peace. I just made it in time.") On that earlier occasion, while the enemy was dividing Gaul into two parts, Beckett had holed up in his flat in the fifteenth *arrondissement* of Paris and undertaken a heroic feat of pedantry, filling sheets of paper with a French translation of the novel he had gotten published, amid total public indifference, in 1938. This was a more unlikely project than it sounds. The English *Murphy*, portions of which James Joyce knew by heart, consists of some 70,000 words tessellated into a sort of learned language, with glazed austerity and a conjuror's resourcefulness:

"Another semitone," said Neary, "and we had ceased to hear."

"Who knows but what we have?" said Wylie. "Who knows what dirty story, what even better dirty story, it may be even one we have not heard before, told at some colossal pitch of pure smut, beats at this moment in vain against our eardrums?"

"For me," said Neary, with the same sigh as before, "the air is always full of such, soughing with the bawdy innuendo of eternity."

Devising an equivalent for that in the tongue of Racine—"bruissant des vieilles équivoques où s'ennuie l'éternité"—occupied the dark half of Beckett's mind between 1940 and 1942, while the German occupation set up its machinery. A similar temperament, given a slightly different distribution of talents, might have engaged in a piece of prolonged mathematical research, as exact and disinterested, say, as Molloy's statistical treatment of eructation. ("I am ashamed to tell to how many places of figures I carried these computations," wrote Newton recalling a summer of plague, "having no other business at the time.") His daylight mind, meanwhile—that is to say, the portion of his being attested to by *cartes d'identité*—was active in the affairs of the Resistance, in collaboration with his friend Alfred Péron.[1] Péron was arrested, and vanished, as it proved, forever; the Gestapo interested itself in Samuel Beckett; he left Paris "because of the Germans" ("peu avant l'arrivée chez lui de la Gestapo," says a French journalist) and "from pillar to post" in the unoccupied zone composed a second novel in English, *Watt*: Dublin and environs, larger, vaguer, dimmer, and more portentous than life, remembered from makeshift quarters at Rousillon in the Vaucluse, and filled by the diligent remembering mind with a fantastic clockwork of circumstantiality. Pages of *Watt* exceed, with increased tension, the virtuosity of *Murphy*:

---

[1] Péron and Beckett met at the École Normale Supérieure, where Beckett was Lecteur d'Anglais for two years after his 1927 graduation from Trinity College. Péron subsequently spent a year at Trinity when Beckett returned there in 1931 to take his M.A.

That, replied Louit, is the bold claim I make for my friend, in whose mind, save for the pale music of innocence you mention, and, in some corner of the cerebellum, where all agricultural ideation has its seat, dumbly flickering, the knowledge of how to extract, from the ancestral half-acre of moraine, the maximum of nourishment, for himself and his pig, with the minimum of labour, all, I am convinced, is an ecstasy of darkness, and of silence.

Other pages of *Watt* seem to have been written out in a trance of obligation, like some schoolroom imposition—

Here he stood. Here he sat. Here he knelt. Here he lay. Here he moved, to and fro, from the door to the window, from the window to the door; from the window to the door, from the door to the window; from the fire to the bed, from the bed to the fire; . . .

—and so on for some 400 words, until each possible route between bed, window, door and fire has been traced in each direction. Years later The Unnamable is to speculate concerning a task some master has imposed, a pensum to perform "as a punishment for having been born perhaps," which entails the writing out of some thousands of words before he will perhaps be allowed to conjure with words no more. If *Watt* is in part such a pensum, it is also in part the subsumption of distant memories into a style, the withdrawal of candlestickmaker's reality from a place and time now unattainable: Ireland, where old men sit on benches and strange men in lonely houses employ servants, and words are incessantly agitated and the mind is never still. This Ireland, at Roussillon between 1942 and 1944, Beckett delivered over from the remembered realm of irreducible being to the mental world where logic mimes the possibility of order and sentences linked less certainly to fact than to one another move unimpeded through the dark. As with the French translation of *Murphy*,

Beckett set aside the unpublished manuscript of *Watt*, for ten years as it proved.

These things he had done in France during the war, estranged from the home. In the first postwar silence of 1945 he spent a month in Ireland with his mother. Then, homeless still, he made his way through Normandy back to Paris, reclaimed his old flat, and commenced the siege in the room that was to last until 1950.

It was during this six-year siege that he wrote nearly everything that has made his name celebrated, and much else, all of it in French. ("I just felt like it. It was a different experience from writing in English.") Each year he made his way out of Paris to Ireland for a month. Then in 1950 his mother died and the intermittent séance suddenly ended. Since the war he had published one book, the French *Murphy* in 1947, with its dedication to Alfred Péron. His drawer was filled with manuscripts: the English *Watt*, souvenir of the Occupation, and in French four novels, two plays, four tales, and a sequence of thirteen "textes pour rien." The first novel, *Mercier et Camier*, the first play, *Eleutheria*, and one of the stories, "Premier Amour," were jettisoned. The rest, after detailed revision, the minuteness of which can be gauged from earlier versions in magazines, were published, more or less in the order of composition, at yearly intervals from 1951 to 1955: *Molloy, Malone Meurt, En Attendant Godot, L'Innommable, Watt* (out of sequence), *Nouvelles et Textes Pour Rien.*

En Attendant Godot made him very famous. Since then he has dodged the commitments of fame and the Literary Life as successfully as he dodged the Occupation, and from not dissimilar motives. Oscillating between the flat and an outpost "in the Marne mud," he wrote in 1956 his most remarkable single work, *Fin de Partie,* and for three more years busied himself dividing the universe of the novels into radio plays, for voices, and mimes, for no voice. Each time the circle tightens, the equation grows more compact. The first radio play carries us to and fro along miles of road, and employs a cast of eleven. The second confines us within the echoing skull of a single man sitting half an hour in a spot from which he barely stirs. Yet we move at the bidding of this man's imagination along the strand, around the bay, to bus stops and riding lessons, from a bleak afternoon to a crystalline winter's night, from Henry and Ada's problems to the cruel impasse of two perhaps imagined old men in a perhaps remembered great house, back years in time and forward to an interminable future. Henry, in *Embers*, murmuring on the strand, is as much the cheated king of infinite space as the man who sat in a Paris room writing the thousands upon thousands of words of a three-volume novel: for this space is curved, and returns upon itself. And that same man in turn has written the words Henry murmurs, driving headlong, by successively minuter increments, to wedge his art in a cleft where it need never stir more: the Comedian of the Impasse, genial to the last, the ever-receding last.

His one certain principle is that every work is wrested from the domain of the impossible. Let him by his previous operations have thoroughly salted some trampled patch of ground, and it is there that in time of frost he will plant his next seed. If one thing was clear to him in April 1958, it was that *The Unnamable* and the *Textes Pour Rien* had placed him in an impasse where he could not possibly write another novel. Accordingly in January 1961 he published a sort of novel, *Comment C'est*. There is neither preversity here, nor inadvertence, but stubborn policy. But let him explain it.

Chronology

Biographical Data

1906   Samuel Beckett born in Dublin

1927   B.A. in French and Italian, Trinity College, Dublin.

1928-30   Lecteur d'Anglais, École Normale Supérieure, Paris.

1931   M.A., Trinity College

1931-32   Lecturer in French, Trinity College.

1932-36   Wanderings in London, France, Germany.

1937   Settled in Paris.

Work

Date of Writing	Date of Publication
1930	*Whoroscope* (poem)
1931	*Proust*
1934	*More Pricks than Kicks* (stories)
1936	*Echo's Bones* (poems)
1938	*Murphy* (in English)
1940-42 Translated *Murphy* into French.	
1942-44 *Watt* (in English)	
1945 *Mercier et Camier* (Novel—in French)	
1945-46 *Nouvelles*— ("La Fin," "L'Expulsé," Le Calmant," "Premier Amour"—in French)	

1947	*Eleutheria* (play—in French)	*Murphy* (in French)
1947-49	*Molloy* (in French) *Malone Meurt* (in French) *En Attendant Godot* (in French) *L'Innommable* (in French)	
1949-50	*Mexican Poetry* (translations)	
1950	*Textes Pour Rien* (in French)	*Molloy* (in French)
1951		*Malone Meurt*
1952		*En Attendant Godot*
		L'Innommable
1953		*Watt* (in English)
		Waiting for Godot
1954		*Nouvelles et Textes Pour Rien*
1955		*Molloy* (in English)
1956	*Fin de Partie* (in French) *All That Fall* (in English)	*Malone Dies*
1957	Translated *Endgame* into English	*Fin de Partie* *All That Fall*
1958	*Krapp's Last Tape* (in English)	*Endgame* *The Unnamable* *Mexican Poems* *Krapp's Last Tape*
1959	*Embers* (in English)	"Texts for Nothing I" *Gedichte* (including *Echo's Bones*, twelve French poems written 1937-39, and six written 1947-49).

| 1960 | *Comment C'est* (in French) | *Embers*
Krapp's Last Tape and Other Dramatic Pieces (also includes *Embers*, *All That Fall*, and two *Mimes*). |
| 1961 | *Happy Days* (play— in English) | *Comment C'est*
Happy Days |

He has made just one public appearance to discuss the theory of these operations. Economically disguised as an Irish pawn who quails before a Frenchman's dialectic, he played in 1949 the straightman's role in three dialogues with Georges Duthuit, on three modern painters. At the end of each dialogue he is browbeaten into silence; at one point a peroration by Duthuit concerning "desire and affirmation, ... that which is tolerable and radiant in the world" expends its force against a *nolo contendere* denoted by the stage direction: "B.— *(Exit weeping)*." It is B. who leads the dialogues, nevertheless. Sacrificing with exquisite pertinacity piece after piece, he achieves the bare board of the classic endgame, executes two or three futile maneuvers, and then concedes by prearrangement, with the air of one satisfying Necessity.

The opening (B. to play) establishes painter #1[2] as a man who deserves the best attention of the avant-garde, having extended, as the phrase goes, the boundaries of his art.

---

2 Tal Coat. The other two are Masson and van Velde. This exchange was printed in *Transition 49*, #5.

B.—Total object, complete with missing parts, instead of partial object. Question of degree.
D.—More. The tyranny of the discreet overthrown. The world a flux of movements, partaking of living time, that of effort, creation, liberation, the painting, the painter. The fleeting instant of sensation given back, given forth, with the context of the continuum it nourished.

Already D. sounds like a pamphlet by Sir Herbert Read, and B. with a few more moves is able to expand his own opening remark, "Question of degree," into a claim that the revolution in question is insufficiently bleak, is in fact the sort of revolution that the critical bureaucracy (ably imitated by D.) can always be counted on to back. It is simply painting adapted to a changed environment, its goal still the "expression of experience" (whatever these terms may mean), its "tendency and accomplishment" still "fundamentally those of previous painting, straining to enlarge the statement of a compromise."

In so belittling enlargement B. plays the clown. The clown enlarges no statement. He is appalled by competence in all its forms; the whip does not frighten him so much as the ringmaster's infallible skill at cracking it. In his alarm at the human ability to specialize itself, he attempts no rejoinder. Besieged by crashing eloquences, he shrugs, walks off, and leaves their advocates to foam and menace, arrange props, collect gate receipts, cite chapter and verse, confer at the summit, see to the plumbing, and otherwise engorge the world. Leonardo too did all that. "What we have to consider in the case of the Italian painters is not that they surveyed the world with the eyes of building contractors, a mere means like any other, but that they never stirred from the field of the possible, however much they may have enlarged it." And today's revolutionary art simply continues their endeavors:

B.—The only thing disturbed by the revolutionaries Matisse and Tal Coat is a certain order on the plane of the feasible.

D.—What other plane can there be for the maker?

B.—Logically none. Yet I speak of an art turning from it in disgust, weary of its puny exploits, weary of pretending to be able, of being able, of doing a little better the same old thing, of going a little further along a dreary road.

D.—And preferring what?

B.—The expression that there is nothing to express, nothing with which to express, nothing from which to express, no power to express, no desire to express, together with the obligation to express.

Shakespeare's powers of expression, it is safe to remark, were infallibly equal to his needs, chiefly since what was needed to write *Hamlet* was power of expression. But set Shakespeare the problem of writing a play about the non-appearance of his hero (for whom two tramps are waiting), or restrict him to four characters, two legless, the third immobilized, the fourth dim, and Shakespeare in the course of attuning himself to this assignment would of necessity allow his vast abilities to wither, cease desiring this man's art and that man's scope, and relinquish the satisfactions (such as he found them) of Promethean competence.

So D. in the second dialogue produces a painter who has assigned himself the void in some such way, one concerned with "inner emptiness, the prime condition, according to Chinese aesthetics, of the act of painting." But B. will not so easily be appeased. He discerns, in this man's hunger after a stripped art, two familiar maladies, "the malady of wanting to know what to do and the malady of wanting to be able to do it." Even absence, emptiness, becomes something to be possessed: "So forgive me if I relapse . . . into my dream of an art unresentful of its superb indigence and too proud for the farce of giving and receiving."

With the third dialogue (on Bram van Velde, whom Beckett has championed since the mid-1930's) the clown takes an offensive of sorts. He defines the Beckett/van Velde situation and act:

> The situation is that of him who is helpless, cannot act, in the end cannot paint, since he is obliged to paint. The act is of him who, helpless, unable to act, acts, in the event paints, since he is obliged to paint.
> D.—Why is he obliged to paint?
> B. I don't know.
> D.—Why is he helpless to paint?
> B.—Because there is nothing to paint and nothing to paint with.

(What this can mean we see at last ten years later in *Comment C'est*.) Thus the painting of B's predilection is "bereft of occasion in every shape and form, ideal as well as material": is pure act, we may say, by pure inaction. As negative and positive numbers are equally infinite, it approaches through sheer incapacity the Cartesian angelism, devoid of occasions, subjects, objects, relations, evading the elaborate mysteries of cognition and of the interaction between mind and hand. (Descartes evaded them, speculatively.) This is easy for common sense to refute; D. refutes it: "But might it not be suggested, even by one tolerant of this fantastic theory, that the occasion of his painting is his predicament, and that it is expressive of the impossibility to express?"

By now the form D. would impose on this discourse grows clear. It resembles an endless algebraic fraction, the denominator splintering itself an infinite number of times. Discard qualities for art to seek after, and the fact that you discard them becomes itself a quality to be sought after. B. assails this very principle. For such an artist, obsessed with possessiveness, obsessed with his expressive vocation, "anything and everything is doomed to become occasion, including . . . the pursuit of occasion. . . . No painting is more replete than Mondrian's." For such an artist, consequently, art always fails; his wooing of the occasion, however sophisticated, is "shadowed more and more darkly by a sense of invalidity, of inadequacy, of existence at the expense of all that it includes, all that it blinds to." And so "the history of painting, here we go again, is the history of its attempts to escape from this sense of failure, by means of more authentic, more ample, less exclusive relations between representer and representee, in a kind of tropism towards a light of which the best opinions continue to vary, and with a kind of Pythagorean terror, as though the irrationality of pi were an offense against the deity, not to mention his creature."

The terrified Pythagoreans blocked number science for a long time. Starting from the faith that the system of rational numbers and the system of the visible world can be made to express one another, they had happily complicated their computations to accord with more complicated data, until it suddenly became evident that the diagonal of a square, let the computer twist and turn as he please, is simply incommensurate with its side. Immediately such incommensurables as $\sqrt{2}$ became the subject of a cult of secrecy. Initiates were sworn not to divulge their existence to outsiders; and they were named *Alogon*, the Unnamable, a fact which links Beckett's most forbidding novel with his first and most inviting, the protagonist of which, Murphy, is freely called "a surd." (Early in *Murphy* we are advised of the retribution visited on one Hippasos "for having divulged the incommensurability of side and diagonal." Eleven years and a war separate this remark from the dialogues with Duthuit; Beckett's preoccupations are surprisingly stable.)

The implication, advanced with Hibernian insouciance, is that prose fiction has hitherto been operated like a Pythagorean cult, in a conspiracy of silence concerning its own incapacity. Beckett's people meanwhile, not through some freak of maladjustment, not on account of their superior endowments (they have none), are radically and metaphysically unassimilable, a fact corresponding to their role as tramp-philosophers. They will not fit into some vast social or fictional machine, as Joyce (who carried traditional procedures to their ultimate) fitted Leopold Bloom. Nor, in the late phases of the enterprise, will they fit into any known world. It is by program a fiction of outcasts.

At the close of the three dialogues B. makes no such ringing assertion, either about Samuel Beckett's fictions or about his friend van Velde's paintings. True to the clown's role, he simply recants, by prearrangement ("Yes, yes, I am mistaken, I am mistaken.") and slips away. Beckett's work, however, incorporates such an assertion, if it incorporates anything or asserts anything; and the parallel with Joyce, Beckett developed on another occasion, noting that whereas "the more Joyce knew the more he could," this tendency towards omniscience and omnipotence need not exhaust art. "I'm working with impotence, ignorance. I don't think impotence has been exploited in the past."

The clown exploits impotence, to be sure, when he allows to bubble up into sustained mimetic coherence his own inability to walk a tightrope, missing his footing, misplacing but never dropping his bowler hat (which catches on a button behind his collar and, obeying immutable mechanical laws, is carried round out of reach as he turns to clutch at the space where it was), collapsing in an arc which carries his hands exactly to a graspable stanchion, retarding his pace to zero for long reflection, crowding six desperate acrobatic movements into a split second. He does not *imitate* the acrobat; it is plain that he could not; he offers us, directly, his personal incapacity, an intricate art form. The man who imitates is the acrobat himself (all ropewalkers are alike), adding to what we have seen before in other circuses some new minuscule difficulty overcome, moving on felt-shod feet a little further along the dreary road of the possible.

4

Let us look at this analogy a while longer.

There is something mechanical about ropewalker's skill. Perpetually improving his technique, he moves step by step toward what Wyndham Lewis called "the sleep of the machine." A perfect, a gyroscopic, cessation of consciousness and suppression of personality could do his work perfectly, as the camera depicts or the computer figures. Alas, being conscious, being a human person, he writes things like *The Odyssey* or *The Divine Comedy*, to tease a successor into emulation. Or, succeeding himself, he writes out the pages of *Watt* that postulate, for example, a man, a door, a fire, and a window and, exhausting by system every possible relation between them, leaves nothing for a successor to do.

Clown on the contrary knows that ideal ropewalking is impossible, certainly for him; his theme, his material, is its impossibility, his incapacity; if being conscious stands in his way, he will focus on that; he will be comically, superabundantly conscious, supernally resourceful, frantically methodical, the more so as he settles his features more and more into the lineaments of the ideal mechanical sleep: the immobility of The Unnamable, or of blind Hamm in his great castered chair.

Ropewalker too becomes absorbed with consciousness. The novelist (again!) lives in the act of writing, so ropewalker discerns bitterly, as consciousness in the act of thinking. If he proposes to stop writing of himself, thinking of himself, himself entertaining such a proposition becomes in turn a theme for writing or an object of thought. (This is the scenario of the *Textes Pour Rien*.) Just in this manner the three dialogues with D. disclosed to B. an infinite perspective of checkmates. If you play chess against yourself you will always lose, though you may conceivably postpone the end of the game forever.

Ropewalker, though he keeps on, despairs, and for ample reasons. Clown mimes despair, transforming it into an exquisite ceremony. Beckett, in various books, has played both roles, gradually working, by rigorous maneuvers, toward the clown's poise and amplitude. There are books— *Proust, More Pricks Than Kicks,* and various collections of poems—in which he is not clear whether he is a comic writer or simply a bitter one, and his first comic book, *Murphy*, achieves its daft freedom in a kind of air pocket, while simultaneously poems written in French precipitate into three or four hundred words his mounting nausea with the human state.

He has had a difficult development, for he has taken on himself the burden of one conscious that he is conscious, since the seventeenth century a peculiarly Western burden. That is the meaning of his stories within stories, his plays within plays, his characters within characters. It is also, with its eerie fidelity to the movements of a mind that has noted itself in motion, the point where his highly specialized, self-immolating art impinges on our sense of the familiar. When we find Molloy momentarily forgetting who he is and strutting before himself (his phrase) like a stranger, or reflecting on the exact sense of such an expression as "I said to myself," we may be startled as by a violation of our own privacy: we recall not so much doing such things as catching ourselves doing them. From such arabesques it is but a step, in principle, to the spectacle of Malone in bed proposing to be

present at his own death (we all await death), and distract-
ing himself meanwhile by telling himself stories, notably
the biography of Macmann, whose death he hopes to syn-
chronize with his own. Beckett protagonists characteristically
tell themselves stories, and the boundary between fiction and
experience is impossible to fix. The whole, in turn, is enclosed in Beckett's fiction; and from the unsettling intimacy
of these works with what you find when you think about
yourself, their magnetic power emanates. By the end of the
trilogy our attention is being held by nothing succulent, no
narrative, nothing but the turning wheels of rigorous precision. It has spiraled inward—

> Where now? Who now? When now? Unquestioning. I,
> say I. Unbelieving. Questions, hypotheses, call them that.
> Keep going, going on, call that going, call that on.

—to the center of the solitary world, the world in which
every man lives nine-tenths of his life alone. It offers
for our inspection, even as we read fascinated, the fascination with sequence, logic, association, with the permutation of our small private stock of ideas, that enables us to
keep ourselves company for many, many years.

The fallacy of most introspective fiction, which Beckett's performance has rendered largely supererogatory, lies
in its too ready assumption that the inherent interest of human beings is self-evident. But it is not immediately evident,
as satirists have been reminding us since Juvenal, that human charm is all-sufficient. The reader of Beckett will understand Wyndham Lewis's claim that the greatest satire is
nonmoral, and constitutes an attempt to understand how
man bears his own company. For that he does bear his own
company, and often gladly, is a fact to be understood, not a
proposition to be established. It is with great difficulty that
Shakespeare's dying giants maintain their own good opinion

of themselves. "And say besides that in Aleppo once. . ."

To purify such vertigo by logic has been the historic work of the great Irish writers, who have always been able to regard a human dilemma as essentially an epistemological, not an ethical, comedy. Swift trapped the reader midway between Gulliver's perception of the Lilliputians and the Lilliputians' perception of Gulliver; Yeats, in "The Phases of the Moon," presents Aherne and Robartes discussing the ignorance of a man in a tower who is meanwhile writing the poem which provides them with the knowledge they are scheming to withhold from him; Joyce placed the dreamer inside his own dream, simultaneously generating and being generated by the voices of all the world. The one certainty from which a reader may start is a mischievously self-sufficient piece of writing, the fuller, perhaps, the emptier. *Ulysses* and *A Tale of a Tub* alike urge on us the existence in our hands of the physical book, a typographical artifact which is somehow "about" its own existence. *Ulysses* even contains, as its principal characters, a writer who could not have written it and a reader who would be unequipped to read it, each of them versions, moreover, of the actual writer and the ideal reader. Such works rotate before us a narcissism which entoils our own faculties, and is somehow related to the writer's involvement in his writer's job, and the reader's awareness of this involvement.

They have also all of them what Stephen Dedalus' classmate called "the true scholastic stink": logic, marginalia and cross-references, transposing a tradition of learned manuscripts into that of Gutenberg technology. The Irish, who go constantly into exile, have supplied the Age of Reason and its successors with several reincarnations of the vagrant scholar: Swift, rewarded with the Deanship of St. Patrick's like a twelfth-century clerk with a canonry, or Joyce, after much wandering, the schoolmaster of Paris, with Samuel Beckett, Master of Arts of Trinity College, Dublin, for a time a clerk in his entourage. We are never far, in Beckett's world, from the academic *flâneur*. Mr. Rooney notes that the Gaelic "Fir" on the door of the men's room is "from Vir Viris, I suppose, the *V* becoming *F*, in accordance with Grimm's Law," and with still more surprising accuracy derives "buff" from "buffalo." Moran in decline lists sixteen theological questions that have preoccupied him, notably "What value is to be attached to the theory that Eve sprang not from Adam's rib but from a tumour in the fat of his leg (arse?)?" The great casuistical speech of the vagrant Lucky is staged like a Master's Oral before three examiners—

> POZZO: Think, pig! . . .
> LUCKY: Given the existence as uttered forth in the published works of Puncher and Wattmann of a personal God quaquaquaqua. . . .

And the most sustained set piece in the canon details the performance, before an examining committee, of a certain Louit who has expended a fifty-pound grant, allegedly on research concerning *The Mathematical Intuitions of the Visicelts*, and is now to report on "the impetus imparted to his studies by his short stay in the country," during which, *inter alia*, the boots, "for the purchase of which fifteen shillings had been allotted to him from the slender College funds . . . had unfortunately been sucked off his feet by a bog, which in the fading light, and the confusion of his senses consequent on prolonged inanition, he had mistaken for a field of late onions." On these twenty-eight pages of *Watt* time stands still, and we barely notice the expenditure of six of them on a mathematical analysis of how the random mutual glances of a five-man or n-man committee could, in an ideal world not much different from the one in hand, be systematized so that no looks are duplicated or go astray. Endless leisurely academic procedure ("Sivinty-thray? said Mr de Baker. Perhaps he means seventy-three, said Mr O'Meldon. Does he mean seventy-three? said Mr Fitzwein. He said seventy-three, said Louit. Did he indeed, said Mr de Baker. My God, said Mr MacStern. His What? said Mr O'Meldon. His God, said Mr Magershon.") —this is one mode of an earthly paradise, *in terra Samuelis*.

He remains, until nearly forty, himself the wandering scholar, chiefly in Paris but sometimes elsewhere in Europe. *Whoroscope* (which won a prize for poems about Time) has 98 lines and 17 footnotes, a higher average than *The Waste Land*. Attached to no academy (though he was two years Lecteur d'Anglais at the École Normale Supérieure, and a year back in Trinity as lecturer in French), he published his monograph on Proust, emitted at irregular intervals his landscape poems of an intellectual vagrant (*Echo's Bones*, and others uncollected), and amassed short stories, with mutual cross-references like a set of learned texts, about a Trinity man—solipsist, jongleur, lecher, pedant, poet—named Belacqua Shuah, the improbable praenomen compounded from Dante and gutter-Irish ("Bollocky") : a notably Goliardic assortment of juvenilia.

Uncollected pieces mirror the décor of the international 30's: a "Text" in the manner of Joyce ("Come come and cull me bonny bony doublebed cony swiftly my springal"), poems in the manner of Stephen Dedalus—

> (Fool! do you hope to untangle
> the knot of God's pain?
> Melancholy Christ that was a soft one!
> Oh yes I think that was perhaps just a very little inclined to be rather too self-conscious)

—and stories in the manner of an erudite youth fondling

private jokes. These have all slipped into decent oblivion in the files of *Transition* and the *New Review*, detritus of the mind of an academic bohemian (Dublin, Paris, Frankfort) preoccupied with its own cleverness and inclined toward macaronic effects because (Joyce aside) it is interested mainly in exteriorizing its own processes, which include dexterity with the languages it happens to know: English, French, German, Italian, Latin. Like the uncollected poems (of which one title should be salvaged: "Casket of Pralinen for a Daughter of a Dissipated Mandarin"), the ones in *Echo's Bones and Other Precipitates* (1936) flaunt a Goliardic swing, a macaronic texture, and an insouciant impenetrability, all these qualities numbed by a barely controlled violence of objurgation:

> this clonic earth
> all these phantoms shuddering out of focus
> it is useless to close the eyes
> all the chords of the earth broken like a woman pianist's
> the toads abroad again on their rounds
> sidling up to their snares
> the fairy-tales of Meath ended
> so say your prayers now and go to bed
> your prayers before the lamps start to sing behind the
>   larches
> here at these knees of stone
> then to bye-bye on the bones

Creation has the bad taste to be unsatisfactory.

The Belacqua stories squander comparable ingenuities of expression, ravelling out into (unsupplied) footnotes. We are told, for instance, that Belacqua and Winnie had not been long on the hilltop "before he began to feel a very sad animal indeed"; and the fit reader's pleasure is divided between the impropriety of the information here secreted, and the aplomb with which he has fielded an allusion to Galen's "omne animal post coitum triste est."

Amid sardonic verbal moraines, contrivances of willed absurdity, and bouts of forced laughter, Belacqua ricochets from affair to affair, leaving girl after girl standing in tableau bewilderment, marries thrice, and dies into the immobility toward which all his rampages have been obliquely oriented. None of this needs to be revived, though it is enlightening to know it exists.

These writings turn on a discrepancy between the mind's operations and what the world presents; so it is with no surprise that we discover the protagonist of Beckett's first published book, the 1930 *Whoroscope*, to be René Descartes soliloquizing in a Dublin accent.

This Descartes shares three attributes with the protagonists of the future trilogy: a recurrent obsession (here, about eggs) ; an incapacity for brushing the wing of his mind against persons or things without nausea; and a singular absence of what can only be called identity. He addresses his breakfast:

> Are you ripe at last,
> my slim pale double-breasted turd!
> How rich she smells,
> this abortion of a fledgling![3]
>
> I will eat it with a fishfork.
> White and yoke with feathers.
> Then I will rise and move moving
> toward Rahab of the snows,
> the murdering matinal pope-confessed amazon,
> Christina the ripper. . . .

The "abortion of a fledgling" he castigates in an ecstasy of disgust; Queen Christina of Sweden incurs his wrath because ("matinal amazon") she required his presence

---

[3] A footnote informs us that Descartes "liked his omelette made of eggs hatched eight to ten days; shorter or longer under the hen and the result, he says, is disgusting."

at five o'clock in the morning; as for himself, he is simply the spot where these two and twenty other particular distastes intersect. A year after printing this witty eructation, Beckett (Descartes temporarily slumbering somewhere in his soul) produced his study of Proust, in the foreword of which he announces that the page references are to "the abominable edition of the *Nouvelle Revue Française*, in sixteen volumes."

5

As this exasperation indicates, the Cartesian clown is dormant in *Proust; Proust* is the bitter academic soliloquy of one condemned on this earth to walk ropes. With insinuating candor it tears down the world. Its author (age 25) displays a colubrine suddenness of invective and an odd intense tranquillity of appreciation, the former for the human condition, the latter for Proust, an ideal Proust. A style that oscillates between Pater and neurasthenia delivers the elements of the Proust-Beckett universe, in which "we are not merely more weary because of yesterday, we are other, no longer what we were before the calamity of yesterday"; in which therefore, since he who attains is no longer he who desired, "the wisdom of all the sages, from Brahma to Leopardi, . . . consists not in the satisfaction but in the ablation of desire"; the failure of all human relationships is preordained; and "the immediate joys and sorrows of the body and the intelligence are so many superfoetations," because "the only world that has reality and significance" is "the world of our own latent consciousness." Clearly, Proust writing in bed brings up to date Belacqua dreaming in the shadow of his rock; clearly too, Molloy or Malone writing in bed is a hobo Proust.

Thus all that does and suffers is unreal, harvesting only in its moments of inattention the ingredients of the peace involuntary memory may later recover and illuminate; hence the accessible is without exception disagreeable ("And if there were two things that Watt loathed, one was the earth, and the other was the sky."); and any willed relationship of person to person, here and now, "the attempt to communicate where no communication is possible, is merely a simian vulgarity, or horribly comic." (Molloy has such an experience, with a Mrs. Lousse.)

From this not very arresting disenchantment, reminiscent of the rotting apple Auden at a similar age kept on his mantel at Oxford to remind him of the state of Europe, there depends a further argument both facile and subtle. Since the conscious life is an ignoble traffic with the practical world, what is usually called "memory," the faculty that reproduces those impressions of the past that were consciously formed, can recall nothing but the soiled shirts and half-eaten sandwiches of earlier practical trafficking. To augment the banalities of today, the man with a good memory can summon the banalities of yesterday. But in some inner *"gouffre interdit à nos sondes"* is stored what was never corrupted by practical attention, "the essence of our selves, the best of our many selves, . . .the best because accumulated shyly and painfully under the nose of our vulgarity." But this is inaccessible. We cannot be happy in the present because we must be conscious of it; nor can we normally recall that of which we were never conscious. We can only wait, for death, for Godot, or for the Proustian miracle. For, says Proust—and this is the nub of Beckett's fascination with him—what memory cannot locate, nor the most successful evocative experiment do more than echo, will once in a while flood us by accident, when "by some miracle of analogy the central impression of a past sensation recurs as an immediate stimulus," and opens the inner gulfs.

> The most trivial experience—he says in effect—is encrusted with elements that logically are not related to it and have consequently been rejected by our intelligence: it is imprisoned in a vase filled with a certain perfume and a certain colour and raised to a certain temperature. These vases are suspended along the height of our years, and, not being accessible to memory, are in a sense immune, the purity of their climatic content is guaranteed to forgetfulness, each one is kept at a distance, at its date. So that when the imprisoned microcosm is besieged in the manner described, we are flooded by a new air and a new perfume (new precisely because already experienced), and we breathe the true air of Paradise, of the only Paradise that is not the dream of a madman, the Paradise that has been lost.

One may be suffused for instance by "a sour and distinguished prose, shaped and stated by his mother's voice, muted and sweetened almost to a lullaby, unwinding all night long its reassuring foil of sound before a child's insomnia."

Beckett images have a way of recurring. A quarter century later in *Endgame*, where Hamm's active lifelong denial of love—translating the Proustian apathy into a rhetoric of revulsion—has made everything go wrong, those perfumed jars where the past is sealed away are transmogrified into two ash cans, which dominate the left side of the stage in metallic obduracy and contain his legless parents. His mother, in one of them, is rapt back by a chance remark to Lake Como, and for a few minutes enjoys before our eyes the Proustian bliss ("It was deep, deep. And you could see down to the bottom. So white. So clean."). And emanating from the other ash can the father's rebuke recalls the child's insomnia:

Whom did you call when you were a tiny boy and were frightened of the dark? Your mother? No. Me. We let you cry. Then we moved you out of earshot, so that we might sleep in peace.

Now it is their conversations that trouble his sleep:

> HAMM (*wearily*): Quiet, quiet, you're keeping me awake. (*Pause.*) Talk softer. (*Pause.*) If I could sleep I might make love. I'd go into the woods. My eyes would see . . . the sky, the earth. I'd run, run, they wouldn't catch me. (*Pause.*) Nature! (*Pause.*) There's something dripping in my head. (*Pause.*) A heart, a heart in my head.

Blind, in his rigid chair, he gropes in dreams toward "the only Paradise that is not the dream of a madman, the Paradise that has been lost," or contrives fictions in which he figures as the heartless voice of Necessity striking postures before cringing tenants, rapping out harsh rodomontades in a Paradise that never was.

6

We may call what is set forth in *Proust* the ropewalker's view of life. It exudes such a person's dreary dignity, surveying human experience from that great height which anyone can attain with a ladder, and suggesting that there is nothing much to do but plant one foot before the other, in circumstances where this procedure entails great technical difficulty. It is not a doctrine one would expect to nourish a great comic writer, and indeed it does not. The great comic writer pays it little heed, except when he allows Nell her memory of Lake Como, or the speaker of *Comment C'est* a few images of his past life "up there in the light."[4] The mind that chose to publish this exposition retains its stain, however. To the last his people expect nothing of the practical world, and seek equilibrium in entropy.

Thus Murphy regards the mental patients he is paid to attend "not as banished from a system of benefits" by their disorder, "but as escaped from a colossal fiasco," and is greatly soothed by "the absolute impassiveness of the higher schizoids, in the face of the most pitiless therapeutic bombardment." Thus Watt, the most engaging of Beckett's creations, has the utmost difficulty in accommodating his mind to the most utile objects:

> For Watt now found himself in the midst of things which, if they consented to be named, did so as it were with reluctance. . . . Looking at a pot, for example, or thinking of a pot, one of Mr Knott's pots, it was in vain that Watt said, Pot, pot. Well, perhaps not quite in vain, but very nearly. For it was not a pot, the more he looked, the more he reflected, the more he felt sure of that, that it was not a pot at all. It resembled a pot, it was almost a pot, but it was not a pot of which one could say, Pot, pot and be comforted.

In the trilogy this fluid bewilderment deposits jagged crystals. Thus Molloy rehearses the sensations of dissolution:

> This time, then once more I think, then perhaps a last time, then I think it'll be over, with that world too. Premonition of the last but one but one. All grows dim. A little more and you'll go blind. It's in the head. It doesn't work any more, it says, I don't work any more. You go

---

[4] "and yet a dream I am given a dream as if I had tasted of love of a little woman within my reach and dreaming too it's in the dream too of a little man within hers I have that in my life this time on and off as I journey." We meet the indomitable comedian in the next words: "or failing kindred flesh emergency dream a ewe sheep she would not come to me I would go to her huddle in her fleece."

dumb as well and sounds fade. The threshold scarcely crossed that's how it is.

Thus Malone, exacerbated by padded-cell amenities:

> . . . And indeed the silence at times is such that the earth seems uninhabited. That is what comes of the taste for generalization. You have only to hear nothing for a few days, in your hole, nothing but the sounds of things, and you begin to fancy yourself the last of human kind. What if I started to scream?

Thus the Unnamable:

> In a word, no change apparently since I have been here, disorder of the lights perhaps an illusion, all change to be feared, incomprehensible uneasiness.

Last, capping this increasingly bitter series, the equally anonymous protagonist of *Comment C'est*:

> life then without visitors present version no visitors no stories but mine no sounds but mine no silence but the silence I must break when I can bear it no more it's with that I must endure.

This one at least is capable of finding the Belacqua bliss intolerably lonely. Murphy had no such qualms when, more than twenty years before *Comment C'est*, he first inspected the padded cells:

> The pads surpassed by far all he had ever been able to imagine in the way of indoor bowers of bliss. The three dimensions, slightly concave, were so exquisitely proportioned that the absence of the fourth was scarcely felt. The tender luminous oyster-grey of the pneumatic upholstery, cushioning every square inch of ceiling, walls, floor and door, lent colour to the truth, that one was a prisoner of air. The temperature was such that only total nudity could do it justice. No system of ventilation appeared to dispel the illusion of respirable vacuum. . . .

Though *Murphy* is a genial book, and *Watt* a work whose understanding with the reader is suffused with deliquescent lyricism, the tone of the next three novels promises nothing except that the writer will be released from exacerbation only when he has died, and the reader perhaps when he reads no more. *The Unnamable* ends without even the satisfaction of Malone's expiring "Never anything/ there/ any more"; it ends, ". . . I don't know, I'll never know, in the silence you don't know, you must go on, I can't go on, I'll go on."

This disillusion with solipsist joys is already latent in *Proust*, which is a bitter book, aboil beneath its elegant prose with the violence that contorts the poems of the same period. It is forecast also in "Dante and the Lobster," the opening story of the 1934 *More Pricks than Kicks*. At the climax of this tale the commonplace to which Belacqua Shuah has succeeded in reducing all relations with living creatures crumbles upward to engulf him in panic: he has never before realized that lobsters are boiled alive. One gets used to these things, as Belacqua is used to every other happening, and what you are used to you can then at your pleasure invest with fangless drama, as Belacqua eats his bread with saturnine savagery. ("This meal that he was at such pains to make ready, he would devour it with a sense of rapture and victory, it would be like smiting the sledded Polacks on the ice. He would snap at it with closed eyes, he would gnash it into a pulp, he would vanquish it utterly with his fangs.") But the boiling of the lobster, raping his consciousness, is excruciating like all the facts habit has not yet empearled.

"Have sense," she said sharply. "Lobsters are always boiled alive. They must be." She caught up the lobster and laid it on its back. It trembled. "They feel nothing," she said.

In the depths of the sea it had crept into the cruel pot. For hours, in the midst of its enemies, it had breathed secretly. It had survived the Frenchwoman's cat and his witless clutch. Now it was going alive into the scalding water. It had to. Take into the air my quiet breath.

Belacqua looked at the old parchment of her face, grey in the dim kitchen.

"You make a fuss," she said angrily, "and upset me and then lash into it for your dinner."

She lifted the lobster clear of the table. It had about thirty seconds to live.

Well, thought Belacqua, it's a quick death, God help us all.

It is not.

There have been few inventions in fiction to compare with the voice from universal space that speaks those three words. It is later, soured and personified, the prevailing voice of the trilogy. The genial décor of *Murphy* comes to epiphany as Murphy, in his garret room, tied to his rocking chair ("slowly he felt better, astir in his mind, in the freedom of that light and dark that did not clash, nor alternate, nor fade nor lighten except to their communion. . . . Soon his body would be quiet, soon he would be free."), lightens his incandescent mind by a gentle rocking dissolution; when someone, mistaking one chain for another in the water closet, turns on the unlit gas, and Murphy is set free as he had not foreseen. Well, the tone of the narrative seems to say, it's a quick death, God help us all; and Molloy, Malone and the Nameless One stir in their hopeless beds to reiterate, "It is not."

7

That the tone of *Murphy* makes the claim later so rebuked, is a fact related to its narcissism of style. Though the novel is a vastly smoother performance, the author's mind is no more engaged with human fact than it was in the galvanically disrupted short stories of *More Pricks than Kicks*. Nor is it any more constrained than before or later to assent to the chief assumption of the European novel, that something valuable draws people together. On the contrary, a gaggle of grotesques needs Murphy, or needs to find him, but Murphy, the author's favorite, needs no one and nothing.

Our affection, not merely our admiration, is nonetheless evoked, but by the writing. The book is meant to be reread lovingly, sentence by sentence. The coroner wishes he were on the golf course: "He closed his eyes and struck a long putt. The ball left the club with the sweet sound of a flute, flowed across the green, struck the back of the tin, spouted a foot into the air, fell plump into the hole, bubbled and was still." With two details, the flute and the bubbling, this sentence makes easy jest of its own virtuosity. So does the deft procatalepsis which acknowledges how Miss Counihan's endowments are distributed: "I fear you would not pass through the door of my cupboard, not even sideways, not even frontways rather." So does the dialogue of Wylie and Neary, whose effortless amplitude of diction is neither wholly theirs nor wholly the author's:

> "But betray me," said Neary, "and you go the way of Hippasos."
> "The Akousmatic, I presume," said Wylie. "His retribution slips my mind."
> "Drowned in a puddle," said Neary, "for having divulged the incommensurability of side and diagonal."
> "So perish all babblers," said Wylie.

In this exact, pellucid brilliance of language, each sentence strained and filtered, we discern Murphy, the "seedy solipsist," drifting grotesquely, mutely to annihilation while an assortment of minor characters, each in solemn pursuit of some goal for the achievement of which Murphy is preposterously indispensable, dart after him like minnows toward a piece of bread. For Murphy, who is unaware of the pursuers, the central situation is that his body loves Celia, who wants him to go to work and support the two of them—thereby taking her off the streets—while his mind abhors the complications she introduces into his quest for anonymity, for a state of being "not free, but a mote in the dark of absolute freedom," a state most readily approximated by rocking naked in a dark room in a rocking chair "of undressed teak, guaranteed not to crack, warp, shrink, corrode, or creak at night," to which he binds himself with seven scarves. When he dies, Celia returns sadly to her old profession, and we realize with surprise that she has moved through this highly stylized novel wholly untouched by either satire or sentimentality. In the final chapter she gazes at a kite-spangled sky "simply to have that unction of soft sunless light on her eyes that was all she remembered of Ireland."

> The ludicrous fever of toys struggling skyward, the sky itself more and more remote, the wind tearing the awning of cloud to tatters, pale limitless blue and green recessions laced with strands of scud, the light failing —once she would have noticed these things. She watched the tandem coming shakily down from the turmoil, the child running forward to break its fall, his trouble when he failed, his absorbed kneeling over the damage. He did not sing as he departed, nor did she hail him.

The exquisite poise of this writing, its breath timelessly caught between Celia, the sky, and its own eggshell comeliness, concentrates with rare ease the best of Beckett's first novel. Though frequently he indulges in japes and epigrams, it is the aloof compassion with which Celia is presented that secures the book's flutelike purity. The characters—she is the test case—move unimpeded; they are not dolls, no joke is "on" them, they and the author share a pedantically austere estimate of the vanity of human wishes as they circulate through the plot's extravagant minuet. They don't, of course, exist; Celia is a transparent phantasm, the rest are points to which are tied the balloon strings to their characteristic jests. So there is no rictus, neither a point scored by the author nor a fist shaken in the face of eternity, in what an angrier writer would have contrived for the climax of the book, the reading of Murphy's will:

> With regard to the disposal of these my body, mind and soul, I desire that they be burnt and placed in a paper bag and brought to the Abbey Theatre, Lr. Abbey Street, Dublin, and without pause into what the great and good Lord Chesterfield calls the necessary house, where their happiest hours have been spent, on the right as one goes down into the pit, and I desire that the chain be there pulled upon them, if possible during the performance of a piece, the whole to be executed without ceremony or show of grief.

That his ashes are instead scattered by inadvertence on the floor of a pub isn't a last cruel joke (there is no cruelty in this world of bubbles) nor even an auctorial belch, merely a Quixote-like misadventure which doesn't matter. Murphy wouldn't have minded. One retains great affection for Murphy.

8

Yet *Murphy* is not a typical Beckett book. No reader of his earlier writings would have expected him to be able to deal with a character like Celia, and in no obvious way does the more celebrated later work derive from it.

To write it he simply evaded the madness in himself. To write the later books he confronted this madness. The madness in himself, the emetic hysteria of *Echo's Bones*—

> And the stillborn evening turning a filthy green manuring the night fungus

—went into abeyance with the first sentence of *Murphy*, as Beckett gave himself for the first time to his own vein of rich pedantic resignation: "The sun shone, having no alternative, on the nothing new." This retains, it is true, a juvescent smartness; the bleakness of the trilogy is more casual. But it leads without pyrotechnics into another tranquil absurdity: "Murphy sat out of it, as though he were free, in a mew in West Brompton," and that sentence to a third, and within five pages dialogue has subvened and reached without effort a plane of splendid grotesqueness:

> "The love that lifts up its eyes," said Neary, "being in torments; that craves for the tip of her little finger, dipped in lacquer, to cool its tongue—is foreign to you, Murphy, I take it."
> "Greek," said Murphy.

Yet what went into abeyance as this was written, and 70,000 words as good as these, arranged with a discipline that foreshadows the ferocious discipline of *Watt*, was not exorcised but simply metamorphosed. While the clown's mind gambolled in English, the ropewalker slipped into French; and we find, dating from about the time of *Murphy*, such poems as the one entitled "La Mouche," in which a fly is contemplated with Dedalian morbidity:

> entre la scène et moi
> la vitre
> vide sauf elle

ventre à terre
sanglée dans ses boyaux noirs
antennes affolées ailes liées
pattes crochues bouche suçant à vide
sabrant l'azur s'écrasant contre l'invisible
sous mon pouce impuissant elle fait chavirer
la mer et le ciel serein[5]

Having delineated the beast with precise repulsion, he squashes it, and the heavens, for no clear reason, are reversed in their courses. He is playing God, perhaps, and the fly (sucking the void, sabring the azure) is being made to play man. One cannot tell where the gratuitous apocalypse comes from, nor why the precisions of such special-purpose words as *crochues* and *chavirer* are thought relevant. The fly on the window conjures up a headlong violence which its presence does not suffice to explain, a violence merely latent in the poet; the poem testifies to this latency.

Ten years later, about the time he was writing the trilogy, we find him asking in another poem what he should do without this world, without a face, without questions,

où être ne dure qu'un instant où chaque instant
verse dans le vide dans l'oubli d'avoir été;

what would he do, he goes on, without this silence, abyss of murmurs, without this sky, which uplifts itself on the dust of its ballast? And we have barely time to reflect that the sky is rendered visible thanks to dust, and to wonder again at a seeming irrelevance of specification (why ballast?) before he is answering that as to what he would do without

---

[5] Between the scene and me/the pane/void save for it/flat on its belly /girt in its black guts/antennae quivering wings tied/legs clawing mouth sucking the void/sabring the air crushing itself against the invisible/under my impotent thumb it whelms/sea and serene sky.

all these dull things, why he would do as he does anyhow, peering through his porthole, shut up within himself:

> que ferais-je je ferais comme hier comme aujourd'hui
> regardant par mon hublot si je ne suis pas seul
> à errer et à virer loin de toute vie
> dans un espace pantin
> sans voix parmi les voix
> enfermées avec moi[6]

These are intense but facile despairs. It is when the clown imitates them that they leap into elegance:

> Unfortunately I do not know quite what floor I am on, perhaps I am only on the mezzanine. The doors banging, the steps on the stairs, the noises in the street, have not enlightened me, on this subject. All I know is that the living are there, above me and beneath me. It follows at least that I am not in the basement. . . . Perhaps there are other vaults even deeper than mine, why not? In which case the question arises again as to which floor I am on, there is nothing to be gained by saying I am in a basement if there are tiers of basements one on top of another. . . . There is naturally another possibility that does not escape me, though it would be a great disappointment to have it confirmed, and that is that I am dead already and that all continues more or less as when I was not. Perhaps I expired in the forest, or even earlier. In which case all the trouble I have been taking for some time past, for what purpose I do not clearly recall except that it was in some way connected with the feeling that my troubles were nearly over, has been to no purpose whatsoever. . . .

---

6 what would I do what I did yesterday and the day before
peering out of my deadlight looking for another
wandering like me eddying far from all the living
in a convulsive space
among the voices voiceless
that throng my hiddenness

Between this gallant logical pertinacity and the naked statement that I walk voiceless amid the voices shut up in me; between the clown's endlessly resourceful ritual of incapacity, of which short quotation can impart only a vestigial idea, and the ropewalker's grim insistence that he is moving very carefully with little joy; between the books that mime and the poems that merely state, and state little except their author's want of élan; between these pairs of things there is all the difference art can make.

The passage just cited (it is from *Malone Dies*) was first written and published in French. Art chose for its battleground the French language, into which, by the time *Murphy* was being written, the author's endemic morbidity had transferred itself. The strange instinct that, about 1937, divided the two halves of his temperament, the gentle comedian and the morbid solipsist, between two languages, was obeying a psychic principle not difficult to reconstruct. Between a native language and a language of adoption is a difference not merely of tools but of selves. The words in which I carry on that unending dialogue that accompanies my conscious existence, these words cluster, ramify, and so color the unique person that I am as to precipitate within it what introspection knows as a *self*. ("It's a question of words, of voices," thinks the Unnamable; "the words are everywhere, inside me, outside me . . . I'm in words, made of words.") New words then will seek to precipitate a modified self, though the person is the same. And a system of new words learned later in life with the assistance of the disciplined understanding will attract, if they are allowed to invest the consciousness, whatever potential selfhood floats closest to the ratiocinative. (And we may note in passing how Beckett's French keeps recalling the systematic drill of the classrooms in which it was learned: "Elles n'ont pas germé. . . . Si elles devaient

germer elles auraient germé. Elles ne germeront jamais.")
It is perhaps not impertinent to speculate that a precocious
morbidity in our author did not mature or assimilate but
hung in the pit of his psyche, indigestible; that so long as
he was a monolingual writer it infected his words with
frenzy; that he was freed to pursue in English the gentle
career of Murphy when this clot of despairs had begun
speaking French; and that in writing the trilogy in French
a decade later he was facing it down on what had become its
home ground, as Moran in the first division of the trilogy
hunts down Molloy.

Molloy and Moran are more or less the author's Irish
and French selves respectively. The former, wild and er-
ratic, moves on "the island" in the vicinity of Bally, a
town whose name is half Irish cliché, half English obscenity. The latter, prim and constrained, with his chickens
and his parish priest, hails from a Turdy which suggests
not only a second Anglo-Saxon obscenity but the Tour
Eiffel. The hunt ruins Moran forever (there are to be
no more books like *Murphy* and *Watt*), but the writer
has thenceforward the freedom, in whatever he does, of
his whole personality.

Not that his "ideas" enlarge, only his powers. About
our situation Beckett has as little that is interesting or
useful to tell an interviewer as, probably, Shakespeare
would have had to say had the question been put to him.
And what little he seems to say is especially unwelcome
because we sense that it has been arrived at with exces-
sive facility, by giving temperament rein. "Les absents
sont morts," says one of the poems for instance, "les présents
puent," so "bouffe brûle fornique crève seul comme devant."
But the author of the plays and novels does not offer us
a statement. He offers rather to set before us a leaping mind
encased in ignorances very like our own, and to let that

mind, Molloy's or Malone's or Didi's or Gogo's or Hamm's, pantomime its own (our own) incapacity for reposing in stable conclusions. The ropewalker we admire with some distaste, unless he spice his performance with danger (a very high rope, for instance, which makes no real difference to what he *does*.) But to the clown, whatever his despairs, our hearts go out in what one reviewer well called "profound and sombre and paradoxical joy."

9

Before this decisive confrontation with the specter, he achieved one last tour de force in Anglo-Irish. This is *Watt*, where the inhabitants of the daylight world are banished at the outset to a farcical distance, exchanging conversation like this:

> These northwestern skies are really extraordinary, said Goff, are they not.
> So voluptuous, said Tetty. You think it is all over and then pop! up they flare, with augmented radiance.

Watt makes his appearance in this slapstick setting. "Tetty was not sure whether it was a man or a woman. Mr Hackett was not sure that it was not a parcel, a carpet for example, or a roll of tarpaulin, wrapped up in dark paper and tied about the middle with a cord." They are asking in fact the sort of question Watt is later to ask with more mournful tenacity: what? And if, as seems probable, the tireless explicitness of the book is indebted to certain premises of Ludwig Wittgenstein,[7] then the protagonist's name seem a compromise between What and Witt.

---

[7] The father of Logical Positivism, for whom, as for Watt, "to distinguish between what can be said about an event and what the event *really* means is sheer nonsense." See Jacqueline Hoefer's article on *Watt* in *Perspective*, Autumn 1959.

Having established the fact that the external Watt stumbles like an animated parcel through the world of policemen, love verses, hunchbacks, trams, births, and other vaudeville paraphernalia, the narrative settles down lovingly amid the shifting landscapes of the internal Watt, where all is a vagueness, a questioning, a cascade of deliquescent hypotheses. Watt enters, there is no knowing why, the employ of a Mr. Knott. His duties are rudimentary. He stays an indefinite length of time. He is then replaced, as appears to be the custom, and leaves. That is the entire plot, and whoever chooses to see in it a metaphor for human life is welcome to do so.

Mr. Knott is almost as elusive as the deity, and Watt in the Knott-world spends most of his time puzzling over the enigmatic arrangements of the establishment. The remains of Mr. Knott's dinner, when he has not eaten the whole of it, are invariably set outside to be eaten by a hungry dog; and how it can always be insured that a hungry dog will present itself on these occasions torments Watt through four solutions and fourteen objections, until he is compelled to postulate a retinue of at least six famished dogs, "suitably maintained at Mr. Knott's expense in a suitable place in a famished condition," plus five generations of a family named Lynch, maintained on annuities to look after the dogs. After twenty-six pages of detailed speculations, "once Watt had grasped, in its complexity, the mechanism of the arrangement, how the food came to be left, and the dog to be available, and the two to be united, then it interested him no more, and he enjoyed a comparative peace of mind, in this connexion."

For Watt is tormented by a faculty Beckett omitted from the more facile synthesis of *Murphy*. He bears the Cartesian cross, the discursive intellect, with its irremediable itch to think explicable worlds into existence, stumbling through corridors of exquisite absurdity toward some talismanic formula with which it can be temporarily at rest.

> Not that for a moment Watt supposed that he had penetrated the forces at play, in this particular instance, or even perceived the forms that they upheaved, or obtained the least useful information concerning himself, or Mr Knott, for he did not. But he had turned, little by little, a disturbance into words, he had made a pillow of old words, for a head.

Composing *Molloy* in French three years later, Beckett admits no such gentle cadences. What gains for Watt a pillow brings Molloy only protracted irritation, different only in quality from the irritation of keeping silence. He is entranced by some of the details he recalls, his bicycle horn for example ("If I were obliged to recall, in a roll of honour, those activities which in the course of my interminable existence have given me only a mild pain in the balls, the blowing of a rubber horn—toot!—would figure among the first."). But his characteristic tone is the one that dominates his account of his one love affair: "A mug's game in my opinion, and tiring on top of that, in the long run. . . . We met in a rubbish dump, unlike any other, and yet they are all alike, rubbish dumps, I don't know what she was doing there. I was limply poking about in the garbage, saying probably, for at that stage I must still have been capable of general ideas, This is life. . . . Our commerce was not without tenderness, with trembling hands she cut my toe-nails and I rubbed her rump with winter cream. This idyll was of short duration."

If Molloy, unlike Watt, pursues no questions, it is because the phenomena of the visible world simply do not interest him. He tired of them, he gives us to understand, long ago.

10

The late novels turn their surfaces, then, from the light, which falls on bodies in repetitious, cyclic, violent motion. (That is all that an orthodox Cartesian is likely to make of bodily activities, and Beckett from the first has found some variety of Cartesianism much to his taste.) One day just before the war he visited a tramp in prison. This tramp some weeks previously in a Paris street had suddenly stabbed him, and left him to be carried to a hospital with a perforated lung, James Joyce in the background placing anxious calls to specialists. Confronting the prisoner, Beckett now gently requested to know why. "Je ne sais pas, monsieur." The Occupation, from certain points of view, was not less senseless.

Revolving such things, the 1948 trilogy draws down suddenly into a spiraling void the wit, geniality, and relatively engaging sadness of *Murphy* and *Watt*. Molloy expends 300 words on a technical account of how a man on crutches, by applying the principle of the pendulum, can severely kick another man whom he has knocked down. ("I carefully chose the most favorable position, a few paces from the body, with my back of course turned to it. Then, nicely balanced on my crutches, I began to swing . . . in an ever-widening arc, until I decided the moment had come and launched myself forward with all my strength and consequently, a moment later, backward, which gave the desired result.") So is the physical world dismissed as mechanism, and cruelty as an incidental feature. "I rested, then got up, picked up my crutches, took up my position on the other side of the body and applied myself with method to the same exercise. I always had a mania for symmetry."

And the trilogy leaves its fastidious stench on the subsequent plays. Though the author resumes his grasp on the handles of practical affairs, and even generates, in the 1957 *All That Fall*, a bleached poetry of mundane fatigue, the memory of that secular dark night is not to be exorcised. There is no literary parallel for the three books in which Samuel Beckett, releasing a certain violence of temperament evident in his earliest works and suppressed in *Murphy* and *Watt*, turned his face away from every accessible satisfaction, even from the familiar contours of his own language, and jettisoning the very matrices of fiction—narrator, setting, characters, theme, plot—devoted his scrutiny (under the sign of Belacqua) to the very heart of novel writing: a man in a room writing things out of his head while every breath he draws brings death nearer.

From that everything flows, including the bedridden Malone's frequent proposal to enumerate his possessions, like a senescent Crusoe. Reminiscence, fantasy, description, reflection, all the paraphernalia of fiction pass through these books with the disarming obviousness of the unexpected. The narrator constantly shifts his focus of attention in order to keep himself interested. That is what the professional fictionist does too, though he would claim if pressed that he did it in order to keep the reader interested. Yet from no one is a reader more remote than from a novelist; the sheer labor of covering pages fills up his working days.

"There's this man who comes every week. Perhaps I got here thanks to him. He says not. He gives me money and takes away the pages. So many pages, so much money. . . . Yet I don't work for money. For what then? I don't know." Thus Molloy on the problems of authorship.

"I have always been sitting here, at this selfsame spot, my hands on my knees, gazing before me like a great horned owl in an aviary." Thus The Unnamable on the mode of fictitious existence. There are lights, there are sounds, but there is no place and he is no one exactly, like a character in fiction, which is what he is, and somehow a projection of the sedentary author's, which is what he is also.

As for events, we have for instance this:

> I have lost my stick. That is the oustanding event of the day, for it is day again. . . . It would of course have been better for me to relinquish my bed than to lose my stick. But I had not time to think. The fear of falling is the source of many a folly. It is a disaster. I suppose the wisest thing now is to live it over again, meditate upon it and be edified. It is thus that man distinguishes himself from the apes and rises, from discovery to discovery, ever higher, towards the light. Now that I have lost my stick I realize what it is I have lost and all it meant to me. And thence ascend, painfully, to an understanding of the Stick, shorn of all its accidents, such as I had never dreamt of. What a broadening of the mind. So that I half discern, in the veritable catastrophe that has befallen me, a blessing in disguise. How comforting that is.

This is no more pessimistic than *King Lear*, and considerably funnier. If Swift's "Meditation Upon a Broomstick" lies behind it, so do acres of fictional moralizing, reams of gnomic self-praise, and bundles of romances chronicling the acquisition and dispersal of portable property, from *Robinson Crusoe* to *The Spoils of Poynton*. The trilogy is, among other things, a compendious abstract of all the novels that have ever been written, reduced to their most general terms.

11

And not only novels; for the trilogy also manages a sardonic counterpoint to the epic tradition of the West, which proved to be mortal, and indeed came to an end (unless we are going to take *Paradise Lost* for a new beginning) at about the time the novel was invented. That tradition started with Homer, who if he had been a twentieth-century Irishman living in Paris, might well have written the first half of *Molloy* instead of what he did write, if it was he who wrote it at all.

What Molloy is writing, sitting up in bed, is perhaps a faithful narrative, or perhaps he is making it up. At any rate, it purports to deal with his journey to that room. He set out, it seems, on a bicycle, intending to visit his mother (also bed-ridden); and he has executed a huge sweep, more or less circular, through the to him known world, in the course of which he has lost the bicycle, the use of his legs, the toes on one foot, everything indeed but his crutches and the will to proceed. There has been a Calypso, named Lousse, in whose house he stayed some months after an acquaintance founded on running his bicycle over her dog. There has been a Cyclopean police sergeant, who threatened him with a cylindrical ruler, and before whom our wanderer altered his fortunes by proclaiming his own name. ("My name is Molloy, I cried, all of a sudden, now I remember.") There have been ramparts, and seaboard privations. He had just reached the point when it was impractical to drag himself further on his stomach, and was considering rolling, when help mysteriously arrived.

The narrative is now assumed by a certain Moran. He also is writing, and his story follows Molloy's about as faithfully as Virgil's followed Homer's. Like Virgil, he also imparts a notably administrative tone, being (unlike Molloy, or Homer) a citizen of a substantial community. ("I have a huge bunch of keys, it weighs over a pound. Not a door, not a drawer in my house but the key to it goes with me, wherever I go.") He is writing the narrative of a journey, by bicycle and on foot, accompanied by his son, which was meant to be a search for Molloy, but which in fact brought him back to his own house, minus son and bicycle, crippled, stripped, discredited, and barely distinguishable from his quarry.

So much for the *Odyssey* and *Aeneid* of this new graph of civilization. We next encounter its *Divine Comedy*, which revolves about another man in bed. He is called Malone, at least that is what he is called now, though there are signs that he is a new phase of Molloy, or perhaps of Molloy and Moran together (unless a Molloy is simply what a Moran turns into when he goes looking for a Molloy). Malone too is writing, with a stub of a pencil in an exercise book. What he is writing is an account of his final weeks on earth, and also, by fits and starts, a piece of fiction, to distract himself from speculation about his mysterious surroundings. His narrative concerns a certain Sapo, who midway changes his name to Macmann, ends up in an institution not unlike that in which Malone appears to be confined, and expires at the same moment as his creator.

If The Unnamable, in turn, were Malone dead it would not be surprising. He is seated in a gray space, menaced by mysterious lights, and frantically writing, he is not clear how or with what. He can hardly be Malone, however, since Malone periodically executes an orbit about him. Indeed, he is convinced that all the previous characters are in this place with him, in fact that he invented them and the whole "ponderous chronicle of moribunds in their courses, moving, clashing, writhing or fallen in short-lived swoons." (Were Molloy and Moran, for that matter, fictions of Malone's? Ulysses, it is true, appears in the *Divine Comedy*, and so do Virgil and Homer.) His problem, at the end of this counter-epic series, is to disappear, to cease from being and from troubling, a problem he will be powerless to resolve until he has given satisfactory evidence that he exists in the first place. This is difficult, since he is neither a kind of Virgil, nor of Homer, nor of Dante, but more or less a kind of Descartes (who Boileau asserted had cut the throat of poetry). Nevertheless he too tells sketchy stories, for instance about a certain Mahood who on one leg and crutches executed a world-wide spiraling Odyssey, and on another occasion was confined night and day outside a restaurant in a jar to which the menu was affixed, but despite his efforts to attract attention stayed apparently invisible to everyone but the proprietress. There is an important difference between these stories and Malone's, however, for it is not at all clear whether The Unnamable is inventing Mahood, or whether Mahood is partly responsible for inventing The Unnamable, having told the latter these stories about himself as part of the conspiracy to make him believe he exists. He is locked up with his fictions, at the mercy of an inchoate "they" who have supplied him with the very language he struggles with (yet which of us has made his own language?), and "they" are still perhaps fictions of his, or he of theirs.

Homer, Virgil, Dante, Descartes: these are not continents on a map Beckett has been following; Rorschach configurations, rather, which his groupings of tension and emphasis encourage us to see. They appear because his concentric narratives and serial narrators, each in turn more densely conscious of having had the experience of all the previous ones, succeed one another in the same manner as the major efforts of the Western imagination, each master in turn more burdened by responsibility for the preceding ones, as in Mr. Eliot's vision of The Mind of

Europe. That is why outlines seem to grow clearer and purposes firmer as we work backward: Chaucer was not troubled by reading *Hamlet*, nor Homer by the cosmology of Mount Purgatory. It was the mind of Europe before the mind of Beckett that turned literature toward a more and more intricate self-consciousness, confronting a Joyce or a Proust with an intellectual landscape whose most mysterious feature is himself performing the act of writing. Beckett may be absolved of responsibility for turning even the novel in upon itself. Flaubert's first achieved fiction was a serious and powerful novel about a woman who has become what she is by reading novels.

The plays deal more openly with the past. *Waiting for Godot* reflects in its dusty but accurate mirror the Noh drama (tree, journey, concatenated rituals), Greek theater (two actors, messengers, expectation of a *deus ex machina*), and *commedia dell'arte* (unflagging improvisation round a theme), while *Endgame* beats its bleak light on Shakespeare's stage, dominated by a prince of players named Hamm. Novels and plays alike recapitulate the past of their art, so sparely that if we stare at a parallel it vanishes, so casually that if we ask Beckett the meaning of all this incumbent tradition he can cry with Dan Rooney, "It is a thing I carry about with me!" Yet its presence contributes to the powerful sense—irradiating his inert material—that he has gotten at the form's central sources of energy, and looks into a long tradition with X-ray eyes.

So he propels the trilogy's extraordinary *reductio* for some 180,000 words, incorporating as he goes by the *roman policier*, the picaresque chronicle, the *Bildungsroman*, the universes of Proust and Defoe (these two superimposed), the fiction of self-interrogation. Our attention is held without a plot (a broom that sweeps everything in the same direction), without an undertow of ideas, with a minimum of incident, with no incubus of profundity. What holds us is in part the unquenchable lust to know what will happen in the next ten words, in part the hypnotic fascination of the nearly motionless (flies on a windowpane). Yet he has so distilled these appeals that they operate with uncomfortable immediacy; we are not allowed to suppose that we are reading "for the story," or for some improving purpose. His transparent syntax establishes a tone, a tone of genial resignation, within which the events of the trilogy declare themselves; and these events are small items become momentous, a minute shift of attention, the toot of a bicycle horn, the whereabouts of a boot. For Beckett, manipulating a form that has always indulged itself in copious triviality, has invented for it a convention that can accommodate any amount of detail while rendering nothing too trivial to be interesting.

12

Let us concede that "the novel" is a bore. Wyndham Lewis, the last Titan, caused one of his characters to throw *Middlemarch* into the sea, in default of some appropriate archive. " 'The historic illusion, the scenes depicted, and the hand depicting them . . . should not be handed down as a living document. It is a part of history'—with this he dismissed it." This summary judgment on the trivialities of systematized humanism should jar us into noticing how large an assumption traditional fiction makes about the inherent interest of human beings: people who walk upstairs, walk downstairs, eat eggs, quarrel, marry, converse with clergymen, and ride in trains.

The place of such detail in a work of art has never been satisfactorily explained; Aristotle was not confronted with the problem. Its place in a work of entertainment, however, is a by-product of social history. Defoe filled *Robinson Crusoe* with inventories and iterative chronicles to delight a new mercantile class, who were entranced with the material rewards of self-reliance, and generations of children, who like to tell over possessions. ("Quick quick my possessions," cries Malone, sensing that his time is running out. "A needle stuck into two corks . . . the bowl of my pipe . . .") Subsequently nineteenth-century aesthetics—of the period of Landseer and Rosa Bonheur —certified an art of middle-distance detail as "verisimilitude" (thus defining *veritas*), and nineteenth-century liberalism certified the novel's preoccupation with people preoccupied by trivia as art's truest note, a proper human compassion.

The crucial place of Ireland in the recent history of Western literary art is accounted for by the historical fact that Ireland escaped the humanist dogma. Consequently the great Irish nihilists (for so they appear in a humanist perspective) have been the persistent reformers of the fictional imagination. Swift, a bare seven years after *Robinson Crusoe*, ascribed an overriding concern for footling verisimilitude to a mind so biased toward positivism and so devoid of moral resources that it could be permanently imposed on by talking horses. *Gulliver's Travels* is crammed with inventories and numerical estimates; the narrator's cousin informs us that he edited as much more of the same kind out of the manuscript. The point of so drowning sense in number is to characterize the narrator as a barbarian. The point of the similar exhaustiveness of *Ulysses*, the next great Irish book, is to characterize Mr. Leopold Bloom as a lost mind immersed to the eyes in quantifiable matter. The number of *things* to the square inch of Joyce's text defies computation.

They are the kind of things which are lightly distributed through standard works of fiction to make us feel at home (" . . . a pink ribbon which had festooned an Easter egg in the year 1899 . . ."), and in *Ulysses* they comprise not a background for human identity but a densely compacted substitute. Two chairs, one squat and stuffed, one slender, splayfoot, of glossy cane curves, set mutely before us the tryst of Marion Bloom and Blazes Boylan, and two pages compiled from a furniture wholesaler's catalogue epitomize the imagined fruition of a human life. Insofar as Joyce had designs on the bourgeois novel, his design was to run it to the ground. And in the great catechism of the seventeenth chapter, from which Beckett likely derived the style of *Watt,* Joyce makes it clear that within the bourgeois novel's vaulted recesses nothing human, unless it be the analytic faculty, can survive.

Watt confirms this discovery; and Beckett's next novel after *Watt,* the jettisoned *Mercier et Camier* is his farewell to the bourgeois novel.

> Why do we not throw away the waterproof? said Camier. What use is it to us?
> It retards the action of the rain, said Mercier.
> It is a shroud, said Camier.
> Do not exaggerate, said Mercier.
> Shall I tell you what I think? said Camier. Whichever one of us is wearing it is as much incommoded, both physically and morally, as the one who is not.
> There is something in what you say, said Mercier.
> They looked at the waterproof. Spread out at the foot of the ridge, it looked flayed. The shreds of a flecked lining, pleasingly faded, adhered to the shoulders. A clearer yellow marked the areas which the dampness had not yet penetrated.
> Could I apostrophise it? said Mercier.
> There is time, said Camier.
> Mercier reflected. Farewell, old gabardine, he said.

The silence lengthened. Camier said, That is all of your apostrophe?
Yes, said Mercier.
Let us be off, said Camier.

When they have walked a little away from it, the question arises, whether anything has been left in the pockets.

Punched tickets of all kinds, said Camier, burnt matches, on the edges of bits of newspaper obliterated notes of irrevocable appointments, the classic final tenth of a pointless pencil, several creased sheets of toilet paper, some condoms of doubtful impermeability, and dust. A whole life.
Nothing we need? said Mercier.
As I say, a whole life, said Camier.

How many thousand affecting incidents does this scene not epitomize and write off? As a few pages of Wordsworth's absorb and supersede a century of meditative Miltonic nature musing, so does Mercier's timeless farewell to the gabardine, and the finely pointless inventory of its contents, subsume three hundred novels preoccupied with bourgeois man's chief good, portable property. A few narrative touches, a little epithetic color, would have shaped us one grotesque incident (*in-cidere*, to befall). But this tableau of Virgilian gravity is not to be dismissed as an incident. Beckett's disarmingly effortless presentation has yielded instead what is virtually a myth, like $E = mc^2$, transparent, static, wholly general. By means no different Dante made Neptune's quizzical glance at the Argo, which any merely vivid writer might have thought to exploit, into a timeless gaze: *che fe' Nettuno ammirar l'ombra d'Argo*.

Into this effortless book there vanish, indeed, the practiced storyteller's repertoire of gestures, never more to exert tension on Beckett's pages: two characters, a journey, a goal, mystery, fulfillment, dialogue and setting, meditation, local color, and major structure. It is a third-person narrative (Beckett's last), and it derives a peculiarly engaging astringency from the fact that the narrator seems not to hear our habitual curiosities, so entranced is he by his protagonists. They meet by appointment and set forth on a journey, we do not know why; before leaving the city they are parted from bicycle, haversack, and umbrella, we do not know how; they return from the country in order to recover these objects, it is not clear under what necessity. That is half the action: hear them discourse on it:

> . . . The things (I say things, for want of a better word), whatever they are, which we believe we need, in order to pursue our journey—
> Our journey, said Mercier, what journey?
> Our journey, said Camier, with the maximum chance of success, these things we had and we have them no longer. Now we placed them in the haversack, as being something to contain them. But on further reflection we have no proof that they are not in the umbrella, or attached to some part of the bicycle, with twine, perhaps. All that we know is that we had them once and have them no longer. And even of that we are not certain.
> As premises go, these are premises, said Mercier.

Back in the city they find the remains of the bicycle, they find the umbrella and lose it again for good, and the sack they do not find. They undertake a new journey, it is not clear where, and are separated, we cannot tell why. They meet briefly a last time, and talk by the canal:

> You remember the parrot? said Mercier.
> I especially remember the hare, said Camier.
> I think it is dead, said Mercier.
> We didn't encounter many animals, said Camier.
> I believe it was already dead the day she told us she had sent it to the country, said Mercier.
> He went a second time to the water's edge. He gazed a

> while at the water, then returned to the bench.
> Well, I am going, he said. Good-bye, Mercier.
> Good night, said Mercier.

Rain falls steadily throughout the book. The locale is plainly Ireland, the city Dublin.

These last pages are steeped in a pathos the origins of which are obscure until we notice how the book works. It works by insisting on the utter reasonableness of everything in the immediate vicinity of the passage we are reading at the moment. The reasoning behind the ritualistic dialogue, as in that of Gogo and Didi in *Waiting for Godot,* is of nearly idiotic transparency, very appealing. And no minor contretemps goes unexplained; when on the second page Mercier and Camier play out for forty-five minutes an elaborate mime of repeatedly missing one another at the rendezvous, their timetables are charted with finicky care. This hallucinatory plausibility, as in dreams, is abetted by the casualness with which, amid our ignorance of many things, small certainties are dispensed: the bicycle, for instance, was a ladies' model, without a free wheel, braked by pedaling backwards. Nor has the narrator shirked formal unity; every third chapter of the book's twelve consists of a convenient résumé of the two preceding, whether to facilitate review, or to emphasize the fuguelike interplay of incident, or simply to make it quite clear that he has not been woolgathering but knows very well what he has just finished writing. Close up, then, we are attended by Reason, Farce (which springs from the forehead of Reason), and Structure, the handmaiden of Farce. But as the book proceeds, the mere fact that we are familiar with more and more of it prompts longer and longer views: and these long views disclose local coherence to be enveloped by the absurd. Two men, for instance, engaged on unformulable business (like ourselves here and now), and surrounded by enigma and darkness (not to mention incessant rain), are squandering their every atom of moral resource on a missing bicycle (ladies' model). So incidents no less trivial than the opening peekaboo become, in the later stages of the book, formidable and ominous. Man's fate, it seems, is to inscribe the figures of plane geometry on a spherical surface. From over his shoulder, we may be heartened by his sureness and finesse. It is when we get a sufficiently distant view of the sphere that we can discern pathos in his illusion that he is accomplishing straight lines and right angles, drawing an accurate map or plotting a reliable course.

These increasingly long perspectives are a function simply of the book's duration. They unfold from the simple fact that narrative takes time. It is usual, in Beckett's work, for the very nature of the form he is employing to effect in this way his most elusive declarations. Late in the second act of *Godot*, for instance, the revelation that Pozzo's satchels are full of sand sets up solemn human resonances, whereas a comparable disclosure early in the play would have been no more than a normal vaudeville detail. So in *Mercier et Camier* our persistent sense that we are on familiar novel-reader's ground, familiar signposts of fiction (dialogue, setting, motivation) always in sight, is constantly menaced by our growing conviction that the book's world isn't contained in fiction's crystal box where all is trimmed and at hand and sensible. The certainties of a form rooted in documentation are slowly eroded by a pervasive aimlessness; and *that*, instead of fiction's familiar positivisms, comes to justify the volitional climate in which the two friends do not abandon their enterprise but simply run down.

On page 266 of *Murphy* Celia is able to identify her

lover's body by a large birthmark on the right buttock, of which she became cognizant on page 29 as a result of the nude Murphy having been turned upside down by a rocking chair mishap early on page 28. But *Murphy* is Beckett's sole exercise, and an anomalous one, in the workman-like linkages of Flaubertian fiction. Such fiction explores a locked world; the world of *Mercier et Camier* is open for miles around, clear into the sunless void, in every direction. In Flaubertian fiction, of which *Ulysses* and *Finnegans Wake* are supreme examples, a myriad of unimportant matters are not scattered like sand over the text but nestle into it perfectly. (They differ in this way from the touches of verisimilitude in less crafty books, which mean to give the impression that everyday untidiness surrounds the action.) James Joyce, who had studied the third chapter in the sixth book of the *Metaphysics*, was aware that if the quotidian is pointless it is far from untidy. He was the only writer of prose fiction to face and examine the fact that all, literally *all*, the details and incidents of everyday experience do in fact dovetail together, in the manner of a Thomas Hardy plot, and that this neatness of fit not only does not have to be imported into "life" by the novelist, but of itself signifies nothing whatever. To any natural happening a cause can be assigned, and to that in turn a remoter cause or causes. These little inevitabilities litter fiction: Crusoe's tool chest contains just what he requires, because he was trained by the civilization that selected those tools. The ropewalker's road of accomplishment leads past *Ulysses* to, if possible, yet denser and more authoritative manipulation of such congruences. And the clown's instinct ("I don't think impotence has been exploited in the past.") is to rid himself of the whole problem.

In *Mercier et Camier* he does this by placing the narrative at the mercy of a craftsman sufficiently bored by idiot consistency to suppress its linkages. This man's relationship to the content of the book is artlessly disposed of in the first sentence: "The journey of Mercier and Camier I can recount in full, if I choose, for I was with them, all the time." His continual invisible presence, he does not mind divulging here and there, was that of creator and puppet master; on the third page of the typescript he reduces the mechanics of an elaborately botched rendezvous to a timetable of unsynchronized arrivals and departures, stares at it, and comments, "What a stink of artifice." In the last chapter, where there are signs that Beckett is tiring of the book, we are surprised by a sudden encounter with none other than Watt, whose only connection with Mercier and Camier is a common authorship. Watt smilingly assures Camier that he knew him from the cradle, whereupon Mercier vaguely recalls a certain Murphy, now ten years dead. "They never recovered his body, imagine." In these intramural pleasantries, which contain the germ of *The Unnamable* ("I am neither, I needn't say, Murphy, nor Watt, nor Mercier, nor—no, I can't even bring myself to name them . . ."), we discern Beckett's sudden realization of the way to lay the present book to rest. If he simply stops writing it he will not violate its decorum, since it has all the time existed, in an essentially lyric mode, as an amusement of its creator, an amusement fiercely pursued. The intensely formal dialogue gratifies his pursuit of form, the descriptive vignettes his taste for silken cadence and abrasive evocation, the arbitrary disposition of incident his somber faith in human orderliness amid perpetual assaults from the irrational. The world of the novel (constantly raining) is the narrator's mental landscape: hence its elusive geography. It grows suddenly clear that we are on the brink of the trilogy; that Mercier and Camier, the narrator, and Beckett who holds the pen, constitute a converging series whose terms are difficult to distinguish; and that this fiction is less close to any other reality than to the mental world of a man sitting in a room before a sheaf of papers.

The Rational Domain

Ah the old questions, the old answers, there's nothing like them!

—*Endgame*

Not count! One of the few satisfactions in life?
—*All That Fall*

1

Let the serpent commence swallowing his tail, and let this process continue to some ideal limit: then ultimately the tip of his tail (who doubts it?) must end up stuffed as far back inside the serpent as it is possible to reach: i.e., inside the tip of his tail. In the same way, Molloy's narrative, composed in bed, of the events which brought him to this bed, must one day be brought down in time to the moment when it was itself commenced; and then discuss the writing of its own first paragraph; and so at last traverse itself to that limit where the writing of the word now being written becomes its own subject. This is what in fact happens in *Malone Dies*, the man in bed writing about himself in bed writing, and proposing to track himself to his own death, so that his last word may be about his last word—better, may *be* his last word; as a spring with no thickness, wound sufficiently tight, will become a point. Malone even introduces a new train of terms to converge on this limit, the sequence of fantasies about Macmann, who if all goes well (and it seems to) will die when he does. The Unnamable, finally, for whom all is always now, need coax no past to catch up with him,

79

nor manage no present *durée* toward a terminus. In that domain where division by zero yields any answer you like, the narrative and its substance grow absolutely identical, and that in which they fuse is pure activity, the ape of pure Act: a going on ("I can't go on, I'll go on.")

A bodily career, then (2) an immobility, then (3) a writing, then (4) a writing about the writing, along with (4a) a fiction arising from and paralleling the writing, then (5) a writing become a writing: this is not only the shape of the trilogy, and by inference Mr. Beckett's Pocket History of Western Thought from Homer to The Unnamable, it has also become an archetypal intellectual career: James Joyce's, for example, driving heroically toward a huge echoing impasse, the introduction into which of any amount of extraneous material will never avail (since I it was who chose it) to transcend the echoes of me. So cartloads of learning, some of it commissioned from disciples like S. Beckett, M.A., will not efface from *Finnegans Wake* the lineaments of the Joyce family, and Mr. Pound's Emperors intimately resemble Mr. Pound.

Descartes himself carried the process as far as 4a, the generated fiction, like the tale of Macmann. For what he does, having brought the narrative of the *Discourse* through wars and wanderings down to the point where he discovers himself thinking, is commence to generate a mental world: for, granted my own existence, then God exists if I conceive Him, and I do; and given the First Cause, I can work out a set of causes; and "examining what were the first and most ordinary effects that could be deduced from these causes . . . I have found heavens, stars, an earth, and even on the earth, water, air, fire, minerals, and some other things of this kind"—minerals, look you, and perhaps even cows, if we can live long enough to work out the details, with the help, alas, of "many particular experiments."[1] Nor will these cows be common cows, but cows begotten by necessary reason, otherwise indistinguishable from the common cows our bodily senses shadow.

This is exquisite comedy, the more so when we look round that century and behold so many homemade worlds, each hung from a simple principle. Give Leibnitz a monad, or Crusoe a chest of tools, and in a little while you will behold yet another simulacrum of the familiar places. So in the final hours of this world's Endgame the blind reasoner and his artisan are creating a hygienic dog. One leg is still to be affixed, and the sex goes on last.

> HAMM (*his hand on the dog's head*): Is he gazing at me?
> CLOV: Yes.
> HAMM (*proudly*): As if he were asking me to take him for a walk?
> CLOV: If you like.
> HAMM (*as before*): Or as if he were begging me for a bone. (*He withdraws his hand.*) Leave him like that, standing there imploring me. (*Clov straightens up. The dog falls on its side.*)

It is Descartes who leads the Western mind to the place where realistic fiction, its accuracy checked by "many particular experiments," becomes a focal mode of art. His journey to the famous room with the stove foreshadows the novelist's journey to the room where one writes day after day, alone. Beckett would seem to be the first to have read the *Discours de la Méthode* as what it is, a work of fiction. In his own memoir Descartes passes more quickly than Molloy over nine years' wandering, "a spectator rather than an actor in the plays exhibited on the

---

1 *Discourse on Method*, Part VI.

theater of the world," but the correspondence remains. He even alludes to Molloy's forest, where travelers, he notes, "ought not to wander from side to side, far less remain in one place, but proceed constantly towards the same side in as straight a line as possible . . . ; for in this way, if they do not exactly reach the point they desire, they will come at least in the end to some place that will probably be preferable to the middle of a forest." He was guided, he tells us, by three or four maxims, the third of which confirms the author of *Proust* in his view of human desire. "My *third* maxim was to endeavour always to conquer myself rather than fortune, and change my desires rather than the order of the world; . . . and this single principle seemed to me sufficient to prevent me from desiring for the future anything which I could not obtain, and thus render me contented."[2] For nothing, he says, was at the disposal of the most fortunate sages of antiquity except their own thoughts, and it is wise therefore to abdicate from the ambitions of the great world. It is all the more wise to so abdicate, when one reflects on the satisfactions to which thought can attain: the child who knows that 2 plus 2 equals 4 "may be assured that he has found, with respect to the sum of the numbers before him, all that in this instance is within the reach of human genius." Descartes' restless mind does not often pause to savor such plenitudes. Murphy, less a conquistador, asks for nothing more.

> His vote was cast. "I am not of the big world, I am of the little world," was an old refrain with Murphy, and a conviction, two convictions, the negative first. How should he tolerate, let alone cultivate, the occasions of fiasco, having once beheld the beatific idols of his cave?

---

[2] *Discourse on Method*, Part III.

In the beautiful Belgo-Latin of Arnold Geulincx: *Ubi nihil vales, ibi nihil velis.*

The beauty of this Latin is highly relevant. Geulincx (1624-1669) was a second-generation Cartesian of whom it is not unfair to say that he moves entranced for 1,500 pages through the balance and ceremony of his own iterations, which uncoil gently like smoke. *Partes Humilitatis sunt duae: Inspectio sui et Despectio sui.* Vales, velis; inspectio, despectio: it is usless to resist alliances that have lain prepared in the Latin language so many ages, now with such gravity to be decanted. The divisions of Humility are two: to inspect oneself, to despise oneself. What Beckett character has omitted these operations, or omits continually to report on the results? "The fact is, it seems, that the most you can hope is to be a little less, in the end, the creature you were in the beginning, and the middle": so runs a portion of Molloy's *despectio sui.*

What especially characterized Geulincx however, and qualifies him for repeated mention in the Beckett canon, is not simply the ceremonious resignation of his prose, but the curious doctrine it serves. It is the doctrine of a "bodytight" mental world, around which, or perhaps attached to which, the body performs its gyrations according to laws the mind need not attempt to fathom. Though he holds it true that we know from our minds outward, we need entertain no Berkeleian doubts about the body; it is real. Nor are body and mind united in the pineal gland, as Descartes supposed; they are not united at all. They are, in the language of *Murphy*, partially congruent, no more. Murphy, we are told, "neither thought a kick because he felt one nor felt a kick because he thought one"; and he was "content to accept this partial congruence of the world of his mind with the world of his body as due to some process of supernatural determination."

All this follows, for Geulincx, from the fact that I do not know how I lift my hand: and *Quod nescis quomodo fiat, id non facis*: because you do not know how it was done, you did not do it. My willing to lift my hand was the occasion for some supernatural agency to re-create it in a lifted posture. Geulincx for this reason receives a footnote in the larger histories of philosophy as the first of the Occasionalists, a school of post-Cartesians of whom Malebranche is the least forgotten. The sun, in the same way, is unlikely to know how it warms me; therefore it does not, though it is true to say that I am warmed in its presence. I move, then, through the courses of my mental life, with which alone I am conversant, bounded by a darkness and surrounded by the corporeal irrelevancies The Unnamable characterized as "moribunds in their courses, moving, clashing, writhing or fallen in short-lived swoons."

Here we have the entree to that strange detachment with which Beckett's people regard the things their hands and feet do: their tendency to analyze their own motions like a man working out why a bicycle does not topple, and their reluctance to live through the senses without scrupulous interrogation of all that the senses report. "I know I am seated," writes The Unnamable, "my hands on my knees, because of the pressure against my rump, against the soles of my feet, against the palms of my hands, against my knees. Against my palms the pressure is of my knees, against my knees of my palms, but what is it that presses against my rump, against the soles of my feet? I don't know. My spine is not supported. I mention these details to make sure I am not lying on my back, my legs raised and bent, my eyes closed." These are strangely contemporary preoccupations; he is like an astronaut in his capsule, referring to gravitation (when there is any) some meaning for "up" and "down." We are all growing used to a world in which long chains of analysis have invaded the most commonplace experiences: motion study, communications theory, motivational research, astro-navigation, these specialisms begin to preempt the plane of behavior on which one makes the bed, talks to one's neighbor, desires a hat, or moves from place to place. The motion study expert can instruct us how best to make the bed in our minds before we make it with our hands, the better to spare the lumbar vertebrae and the metatarsals. By emptying our statements of all content whatsoever, we can build with perfect precision the most general chains of inference, and reproduce them in a computer's switching systems. The very learning process can be programed into branching chains of question and answer, leading the student, like Huxley's young man playing chess with Nature, to an exacting dialogue with an infinitely patient machine. Beckett is the first writer to explore the resources of pity and terror that lurk in a wholesale abstraction now so familiar; he is profoundly right in finding the seventeenth-century Occasionalists aesthetically relevant to an age that has no difficulty in diagnosing their speculative shortcomings.

And science, by no accident, begat science fiction. Since my mental life (Geulincx says) is my own, fiction is its freedom; and fiction, John Locke's anomalous aberration, grows easier to account for than its coincidence with fact. We have seen how Hamm, Malone, and the others continually solace themselves with stories. "Perhaps," thinks The Unnamable, "I shall be obliged, in order not to peter out, to invent another fairy-tale, yet another, with heads, trunks, arms, legs and all that follows, let loose in the changeless round of imperfect shadows and dubious light." These stories draw on what the doctrine of body tightness forbids us to call experience, but only research; in *Murphy* the feminine lead is introduced with a column of measurements, Forearm 9½", Wrist 6", Bust 34", Waist 27", Hips 35", etc. That the stories always run parallel to or converge on empirical fact, as Malone's chronicle of Macmann is asymptotic to Malone's experience of being Malone, is a special case of the Occasionalist principle that mental and physical events are somehow congruent. Physical events in the same way do not interact but coincide. So Watt hears, as in an early score by John Cage, three frogs croaking Krak! Krek! and Krik! at nine-beat, six-beat and four-beat intervals respectively; and one sees from the page on which this is written out how, after a simultaneous start, 79 croaks, 120 beats, 360 occasions taken or not taken, must intervene before the sequence recurs; and how the combination Krek! Krik! occurs seven times, Krak! Krik! four, and Krak! Krek! two, while the unbroken sequence Krak! Krek! Krik! is heard once only. We owe this symmetry to no Ranarian design; each frog attends only to its private schedule of croaks. Similarly we read in *Comment C'est* of a futile ballet on the heath, executed by a man, a woman, and a dog:

> suddenly yip left right off we go chins up arms swinging the dog follows head down tail on his balls nothing to do with us he had the same idea at the same instant Malebranche less the rosy hue . . .

> . . . right about inward turn fleeting meeting face to face transfers and hand in hand again arms swinging silent relishing of sea and isles heads pivoting as one towards the city fumes silent distinguishing of monuments heads back front as though on an axle

> suddenly we are eating sandwiches in alternate mouthfuls I mine she hers and exchanging endearments my

sweet girl I bite she swallows my sweet boy she bites
I swallow we don't yet coo with our bills full

darling girl I bite she swallows darling boy she bites
I swallow brief blackout and there we are again off
through the fields hand in hand arms swinging . . .

This Occasionalist courtship is the type of many Beckett
descriptions—Watt walking, for instance:

> Watt's way of advancing due east, for example, was to
> turn his bust as far as possible towards the north and at
> the same time to fling out his right leg as far as possible
> towards the south, and then to turn his bust as far as
> possible towards the south and at the same time to fling
> out his left leg as far as possible towards the north. . . .
> The knees, on these occasions, did not bend. . . . The
> arms were content to dangle, in perfect equipendency.

Here we have a congeries of gestures owning no intelligible interrelationship, united apparently by happen-
stance like the croaks of the three frogs and only conven-
tionally to be abridged under the concept "locomotion."
By allowing no flow of intention from mind to body, by
positing a succession of supernatural interventions to
bring my hand through millions of ever so slightly altered
interim positions to a place where it can scratch my ear,
Geulincx and his school are driven to a treatment of motion as grotesquely analytic as the work sheets of a Disney
animator.[3] Watt's walking is less something he does than
something we can observe his body doing. "Sicut in omni
corpore sunt tres dimensiones," writes Geulincx, "as in
all bodies there are three dimensions, so in all motion

---

[3] By depriving Mickey Mouse of his tail as a measure of wartime economy, the studio is said to have saved many thousands of dollars: not in
ink, but in time required to keep track of the tail's movements. The
animated cartoon, in which everything must be preprogramed, is
the type of all up-to-date technology.

three tendencies, *abitus, transitus, aditus;* for in all movement there is a parting from somewhere, a passage somewhere, a going to somewhere. . . . . But there is no
departure without transit and arrival, no transit without
departure and arrival, etc." Or again, "Divisio et motus re
ipsa nihil differunt," movement and analysis are insepara-
ble; and the 24 frames into which the movie camera an-
alyzes each second of action correspond to an infinite process
of subdivision performed by the moving body itself.[4]
And since nothing, in the midst of movements however complex, is acting to the slightest degree on anything else,
the parts of the closest description are immersed in a fine
irrelevance: "my sweet girl I bite she swallows my sweet boy
she bites I swallow."

Other things in the Beckett cosmos, in addition to the
pervasive self-abnegation and the analytic treatment of
process, seem sponsored by Geulincx. The most important of these is the voice that injects postulates into the
otherwise closed system of discourse. "I quote," says the
protagonist of *Comment C'est* time and again: *je cite
. . . je cite . . . je cite . . .*; and The Unnamable, who can experience with his eyes nothing but the void directly ahead
of him, ascribes his general knowledge to a shadowy and
doubtless unreliable committee by which he half recalls
being instructed. These authorities derive perhaps from
a supposition of Geulincx, that what he does not know of
his own account he is somehow taught. "There are certain modes of knowing in me, which are independent of
me and which I myself do not excite in myself. They are,
therefore, excited in me by something other than myself
(for it is impossible that they come to me from nothing).

---

[4] These come respectively from the *Physica Vera*, II-12, and the
Annotata ad Metaphysicam, ad II-10.

And this other, whoever he be, must be conscious of this business; for he is the agent and it is impossible that he be doing whatever he does without knowing how."[5] This power of course Geulincx means to call God, transmitting thoughts to me through my body (for what I call sensory experience, since I experience it in my mind, must be called a mode of thought). To this conclusion, however, no Beckett character warms. They find that the body reports chiefly news of its own decomposition, and furthermore they distrust whatever they are not working out for themselves. So everything the mysterious authority has to say is disquieting.

What you work out for yourself, moreover, is fiction: fiction, man's comfort. "I am too nervous this evening to listen to myself decay," muses one of these outcasts from life at the opening of the story called "Le Calmant," too nervous "to wait for the red torrents of the heart's falls, the caecum blindly writhing, and for there to be accomplished in my head the long assassinations, the assaults on unshakeable pillars, the love with corpses." So, "I am going to tell myself a story, I am going to try and tell myself yet another story, to try and calm myself." This man's successor, Malone, takes infectious joy in the processes of fiction. Macmann's coat he describes for a page, luxuriating in the detail of the buttons. The hat next, "marred by a wide crack or rent extending in front from the crown down and intended probably to facilitate the introduction of the skull. For coat and hat have this much in common, that whereas the coat is too big, the hat is too small." Then fiction debouches on fiction, as a consideration of how well coat and hat are assorted leads to the speculation that before they came to Mac-

---

5 *Metaphysica Vera.* I-5.

mann they might have been bought "one at the hatter's, the other at the tailor's, perhaps the same day and by the same toff, for such men exist, I mean fine handsome men six foot tall and over and all in keeping but the head, small from over-breeding. And it is a pleasure to find oneself again in the presence of one of those immutable relations between harmoniously perishing terms. . . ." And lo, we have drifted without noticing, so great is fiction's narcotic power, to the very nirvana of all Beckett lucubrations, where effortlessly the mathematic powers cascade. Geulincx, the imperturable Geulincx, austere as Watt, plays in this way mathematician to Descartes' romancer, not telling us of journeys through woods and evenings spent by a stove, but pouring from hand to hand his graceful abstract sentences forever, their pairs and trios of homonymous terms permuted like the three notes of Watt's frogs. Or he will invest a didactic catalogue with his own pleasure in supple fulgent words: "Video nubes, saepe candidas, nonnunquam atras, interdum quamplurimis coloribus sub vesperam ac auroram distinctas:"[6] Clouds he says he sees, often white, sometimes black; and storms and snow, and smoke and limpid sky, and empty space. But we are not to believe a word of it; it is all words, where we feel his warming presence in this way, words and his pleasure in handling them. As for the clouds and sky, he does not see them, they are exhibited to him. All that he himself does is link word to word, thought to thought, guess perhaps to guess, like Malone lying by the small window beyond which is whatever he fancies. He declares "omnem Actionem meam, quatenus mea est, intra me manere"; all freedom (such as it is) lies behind the eyes. The protagonist of "The End" re-

6 *Ethica*, I-ii-2.

ceived long ago, from one Ward, Geulincx's *Ethics* and a pair of dark glasses, the latter perhaps accessories to the practice of what the former preached. Geulincx was no idealist, and to Ward's death, "crumpled up in the water closet, his clothes in awful disorder, struck down by an infarctus," there clings none of the irony that would have attended the similar demise of a Berkeleian. Geulincx merely shut the domain of the body away, in a gesture mimed by perhaps his most pervasive legacy to the Beckett imagination, a firm, affirmative, slightly narcissistic, functionally ornate, faintly French, Latin style.

2

Let us look again. He is the principal master in our time of the formal declarative sentence, a mastery he has consolidated during his years of writing in French, where one places the subject before the verb and the object after it, and unites modifiers to their substantives with a fragile but inflexible logic. Every such sentence advances the narrative, or the argument, to an exact and measurable degree; there is no ellipsis, no *rubato,* no homely leap of the precipitate heart. The *pace* of this prose is even and indomitable, utterly unrelated to the pace of events. Like cinema it can convince us, despite cuts and flashbacks, that the real is declaring itself from moment to moment, without intervention, abridgment, or acceleration. Hence its suitability to drama, where what happens happens before us now, neither "presented" nor interfered with. Hence, in the novels, its unique identity with its subject, which is not a sequence of re-created happenings but a fondling, by the intellect, of remembered sequence.

Thus Malone, for instance, having just consolidated his belongings, discerns one or two unimportant discrepancies between estimate and tally:

I see then that I had attributed to myself certain objects no longer in my possession, so far as I can see. But might they not have rolled behind a piece of furniture? That would surprise me.

The analytic intelligence examines this hypothesis at its own speed, and with its own criteria of reasonableness. The analytic intelligence then declines to be hurried away from evidence of some complexity:

A boot, for example, can a boot roll behind a piece of furniture? And yet I see only one boot. And behind what piece of furniture? In this room, to the best of my knowledge, there is only one piece of furniture capable of intervening between me and my possessions, I refer to the cupboard. But it so cleaves to the wall, to the two walls, for it stands in the corner, that it seems part of them.

Beckett's absolute sureness of decorum, juxtaposing without a quaver sentences that might have come from the prosecutor's summing up ("I refer to the cupboard.") with scraps of the bleakest notation ("And yet I see only one boot.") presides over a highly formal elegance, into which every qualification required by a reliable formullation ("in this room, to the best of my knowledge . . .") can find its way with scientific precision. No sentence prolongs itself merely because it cannot find out where to end, or is reduced to less than full coherence by human passion however intense. Macmann and Moll make love in a context of bountiful explicitness:

And though both were completely ignorant they finally succeeded, summoning to their aid all the resources of the skin, the mucus, and the imagination, in striking from their dry and feeble clips a kind of sombre gratification. So that Moll exclaimed, being (at that stage) the more expansive of the two, Oh would we had but met sixty years ago! But on the long road to this what flutterings, alarms and bashful fumblings, of which only this, that they gave Macmann some insight into the expression, Two is company.

Macmann's exegetical insight illustrates that of the man in "Premier Amour" whose epitaph, composed long ago, gives him unfailing satisfaction: "Elle illustre un point de grammaire."

> Cî-git qui y échappa tant
> Qu'il n'en échappe que maintenant.
> Il y a un syllabe de trop dans le second, et dernier, vers, mais cela n'a pas d'importance, à mon avis.

And nothing, it seems, can retard or advance the pace of this implacable notation, which ultimately, as one would not expect, sustains Moll and Macmann by the courtesy of so patient an attention. Within this earnest detachment Moll's exclamation loses half its absurdity, and contrives to change from the echo of some negligible novel into an appropriate expression of human passion suffused with human dignity: "Oh would we had but met sixty years ago!" "Would we had" strikes the Roman note.

The Winnie of *Happy Days* in the same way, buried to the waist and later to the neck, maintains a logician's, a grammarian's detachment from her plight.

> Then. . .now. . .what difficulties here, for the mind. (*Pause.*) To have been always what I am—and so changed from what I was.

Though the earth now turns so slowly that through the intensely hot day she feels her body menaced by spontaneous combustion (". . . oh I do not mean necessarily burst into flames . . ."), yet she considers with some agitation whether the hairs or hair one brushes and combs are properly styled "them" or "it" ("Brush and comb it? Sounds improper somehow."), and feels it outweighs the day's miseries to have learned the proper definition of "hog":

Oh this *is* a happy day! This will have been another happy day! (*Pause.*) After all. (*Pause.*) So far.

At her most possessed, she achieves with two dozen words a Calder-like syntactic equilibrium, its parts gently swaying to the rhythm of her consternation. Thus struggling to unfurl her umbrella she articulates in distracted snatches a sentence as perfectly shaped as any in the canon:

One keeps putting off—putting up—for fear of putting up—too soon—and the day goes by—quite by—without one's having put up—at all.

The mind prevising a sentence's latter part, the will directing the sentence past all distractions, the imagination building with just so many achieved sentences as may be needed, these faculties rise over our otherwise benumbing affinity with the animals that cry. A sentence reproduces in slow motion some mental gesture. For the mind to systematize in retrospect its dartings through chaos, and between salient points on that reconstructed trajectory to draw unswerving syntactic lines, is to transfer to graph paper movements the hares and butterflies can only perform. Thus human dignity asserts itself in syntax: a principle abandoned in the English written language some time after Dryden, but still active in French. The regnant principle of English style, a connoisseurship of incandescent phrases, lays an unusual burden on individual words; hence Joseph Conrad's complaint that no English word is a word, that in English you cannot say "an oaken table" without conveying perhaps more than you meant to. You are going bail, in such a phrase, for the table's substantiality, worth, and age. "Une table de chêne" specifies a material and stops. This quality of the language in which they were first composed enters into the very sinews of Beckett's plays.

HAMM: Va me chercher deux roues de bicyclette.
CLOV: Il n'y a plus de roues de bicyclette.
HAMM: Qu'est-ce que tu as fait de ta bicyclette?
CLOV: Je n'ai jamais eu de bicyclette.
HAMM: La chose est impossible.

This strophic exchange is our first intimation that the world is crumbling away on every side of the room where Hamm sits in his chair; it determines, therefore, the rigorous stoicism with which the bleak ambience is to be regarded. This determination the French makes without assistance from the actor. "Il n'y a plus de roues de bicyclette" states merely that from the universe there has been subtracted the category "roues de bicyclette"; it does not posture, it does not declaim. "There are no more bicycle wheels" is unsustained by this philosophic sureness of negation; spoken rapidly, it is overly casual; spoken with feeling, it expends its sonorities in a rhetoric of deprivation, beating fists on an unyielding absence. Translating his dialogue into English, Beckett has had no choice at this point but to use dictionary equivalents, and *Endgame* is noticeably weaker at this point than *Fin de Partie*. Elsewhere, pursuing as always an ideal of impartial exactness, he has had to prune the English very considerably to keep sentiment out.

NAGG: (*geignard*) : Qu'est-ce que c'est?
CLOV: C'est le biscuit classique.

This becomes,

NAGG (*plaintively*): What is it?
CLOV: Spratt's medium.

—a desperate equivalent for the aloof precision of "le biscuit classique." Some minutes later Hamm ascertains from Clov that his seeds have not sprouted, that if they were going to sprout they would have sprouted by now;

CLOV: Si elles devaient germer elles auraient germé. Elles ne germeront jamais.
Un temps.
HAMM: C'est moins gai que tantôt.

There is nothing that can be done for Hamm's comment in the course of transposing this exchange into a more sentimental idiom: spoken English cannot protect "moins gai" with the rigor of the negative comparative, as impersonal as a minus sign, nor prevent "tantôt" from expanding into a yearning after vanished yesterdays; nor can it, for that matter, supply an equivalent for "Elles ne germeront jamais" sufficiently austere to declare its meaning and stop. Determined at all costs to keep at bay a pathos that would ruin the play, Beckett having written "They'll never sprout" instructs the actor to utter this line *"violently,"* and as for "C'est moins gai que tantôt," he has contented himself with "This is not much fun."

It is clear that when he quailed before the prospect of rewriting this play in English and wrote to Alan Schneider that the English text would inevitably be a poor substitute ("the loss will be much greater than from the French to the English *Godot*"), the author spoke the simple truth. This is not the generic problem of "untranslatability," a question of values and nuances. It is a principle entoiled in the very conception of *Fin de Partie*, which carries to one extreme (there are others) the Beckett concern with style as a phenomenon of explicitness, and elucidates his prolonged immurement with the French language.

One side of explicitness is pedantry: that habit of mind which takes keen pleasure not in knowing but in retracing the process of arriving at knowledge. (Virtue, wrote Arnold Geulincx, is the Love of Reason: *Virtus est Amor Rationis*; and by reason is meant the rational process, not the contemplation of its results: *Nam Virtus solam Rationem admittit, solam illam sinu complexuque suo dignatur; omnem aliam contemplationem excludit.*) The pedant is not impelled to use the Theorem of Pythagoras for squaring off a building lot, he delights to savor each of the stages by which the theorem itself is proved: an act of pure connoisseurship, yielding nothing new, one human approximation to the pure intellection of the angels, who make no discoveries. As Molloy describes step by step the Odyssey that brought him to this bed, so the pedant rehearses the past because it is bounded, definite, mysterious yet circumscribed. He is chained to some point of origin, and fondles lovingly each of the links, with a rapture analogous to the mathematical passions. If ax^2 plus bx plus c equals zero, then without fail, exception, or doubtful case x will equal minus b, plus or minus the square root of b^2 minus $4\ ac$, the whole divided by $2a$, and this truth, if it can never expand, can never be worn out. So we are invited to refinger the smoothed formulations of Watt: "Obscure keys may open simple locks but simple keys obscure locks never"; or, "By what means then were the dog and the food to be brought together, on those days on which, Mr Knott having left all or part of his food for the day, all or part of the food was available for the dog?" Or at greater length, and with further nuances of pedantry,

> Now Erskine's room was always locked, and the key in Erskine's pocket. Or rather, Erskine's room was never unlocked, nor the key out of Erskine's pocket, longer than two or three seconds at a stretch, which was the time that Erskine took to take the key from his pocket, unlock his door on the outside, glide into his room, lock his door again on the inside and slip the key back into his pocket, or take the key from his pocket, unlock his door on the inside, glide out of his room, lock the door

again on the outside and slip the key back into his pocket. For if Erskine's room had been *always* locked, and the key *always* in Erskine's pocket, then Erskine himself, for all his agility, would have been hard set to glide in and out of his room, in the way he did, unless he had glided in and out by the window, or the chimney. But in and out by the window he could not have glided, nor in and out by the chimney, without being crushed to death. And this was true also of Watt.

Here, expanded into a kind of aesthetic principle, and equipped with a protagonist to correspond, we have the technical narcissism of *Murphy*, obeying the impulse of every principle in the Beckett cosmos to declare itself somewhere in full and at leisure. Watt, who inhabits the house of Mr. Knott in a kind of weak-eyed speculative daze, illustrates the principle that the pedant is the supreme aesthete (Lyly; Wilde), and so that every use of language sufficiently comprehensive and explicit tends, at the expense of brevity, to aesthetic status. Consider for instance the ten pages of *Watt* that caress the incident of the Galls, father and son. These two appear at Mr. Knott's door, and the younger, a middle-aged man, makes a brief speech of introduction:

> We are the Galls, father and son, and we are come, what is more, all the way from town, to choon the piano.

They already sound as though they have rather invented themselves on the spot than walked in from a busy world. "What is more" is delicious. After the piano is tuned the younger Gall speaks again:

> The mice have returned, he said.
> The elder said nothing. Watt wondered if he had heard.
> Nine dampers remain, said the younger, and an equal number of hammers.
> Not corresponding, I hope, said the elder.

In one case, said the younger.
The elder had nothing to say to this.
The strings are in flitters, said the younger.
The elder had nothing to say to this either.
The piano is doomed, in my opinion, said the younger.
The piano-tuner also, said the elder.
The pianist also, said the younger.
This was perhaps the principal incident of Watt's early days in Mr Knott's house.

Watt, however, cannot forbear to rehearse the incident in his head until it has "developed a purely plastic content and gradually lost, in the nice process of its light, its sound, its impacts and its rhythm, all meaning, even the most literal." It thus becomes—and this receives several pages of study—an incident "of great formal brilliance and indeterminable purport" (like all the rest of the book), so that it is plausible to ask whether whatever happened had actually no meaning in the least at the moment of its taking place: "Were there neither Galls nor piano then, but only an unintelligible series of changes, from which Watt finally extracted the Galls and the piano, in self-defense?"

That things and events are extracted in self-defense from an unintelligible continuum of changes is one of philosophy's self-cancelling propositions, assailing the very act of its own affirmation. It is thus ideally suited to Beckett's characteristic comedy of the impasse. It is first cousin to the statement, "Every statement that I make is meaningless." It hands over all discourse to the domain of Style; terms have sounds but not referents, sentences shape but not purport. Thus Watt begins to communicate "back to front":

Day of most, night of part, Knott with now. Now till up, little seen so oh, little heard so oh. Night till morning from. Heard I this, saw I this then what. Things quiet, dim. Ears, eyes, failing now also. Hush in, mist in, moved I so.

Later he inverts ("with all his usual discretion and sense of what was acceptable to the ear, and aesthetic judgement") not only the order of the words in the sentence but that of the letters in the word and that of the sentences in the period:

> Dis yb dis, nem owt. Yad la, tin fo trap. Skin, skin, skin. Od su did ned taw? On. Taw ot klat tonk? On. Tonk ot klat taw? On. Tonk ta kool taw? On. Taw to kool tonk? Nilb, mun, mud. Tin fo trap, yad la. Nem owt, dis yb dis.[7]

In rhythm, in symmetry, even often in euphony, this is as formal as anything in the book. As for coherence, it obeys the rule that the terms on either side of an equation may be arranged in any order. "I am interested in the shape of ideas," Beckett told Harold Hobson, "even if I do not believe in them. There is a wonderful sentence in Augustine. I wish I could remember the Latin. It is even finer in Latin than in English. 'Do not despair; one of the thieves was saved. Do not presume; one of the thieves was damned.' That sentence has a wonderful shape. It is the shape that matters."

We are back among the formulations of *Proust*. Daily expediency finds one ordering of the sensate tumult convenient, the mind at ease within itself may cherish quite another, and occasionally the two may intersect. No special prestige attaches to any grouping the mind may choose to impose: the odds against any combination of thirteen cards are exactly as great as the odds against thirteen spades. The rules of a game which impute special virtue to the latter (no rarer in itself than any other grouping)

---

[7] Sid by sid, two men. Al day, part of nit. Dum, num, blin. Knot look at wat? No. Wat look at knot? No. Wat talk to knot? No. Knot talk to wat? No. Wat den did us do? Niks, niks, niks. Part of nit, al day. Two men, sid by sid.

simply acknowledge that symmetry is satisfying in itself, and helpful to the memory.

So fact dissolves into symmetry; not that "fact," for Watt, is anything but a collective prejudice. *Watt* touches the unreflecting world at just four points: first, on a Dublin street, where a narrative that began in pedantry ("They sat down beside him, the lady on the one side, the gentleman on the other. As a result of this, Mr Hackett found himself between them.") passes through ceremony to fantasy; second, in the not-world of Mr. Knott, where the episodes of Erskine's key, and the scavenging dog, and the Galls, father and son, are melded in the deliquescent faculties of Watt; third, in an institution for the gently unbalanced, where Watt communicates his experiences to a certain Sam, who assumes responsibility for the narrative in its present form; and fourth, at the station, where in Part I we find Watt detraining for his sojourn with Mr. Knott, and in Part IV we find him to have somehow disappeared. (I omit, as not pertaining to any known world, the book's *Paradiso*, the twenty-eight page fantasy transacted in a college committee room.) Each of these milieux—street, house, asylum, station—undergoes, as did the Galls, father and son, an eerie disintegration into cadence, balance, and imperturbable reason. Imperturbable reason is the soul of pedantry, cadence and balance its ceremonial. They have power to dilute the importunity of things and neutralize the energetic passions. Watt considers at length in what order, if at all, he should shut the door, set down his bags, and rest; and pedantry, having rehearsed every combination of these actions, counsels him to undertake none: "For the sitting down was a standing up again, and the load laid down another load to raise, and the door shut another door to open, so hard upon the last, so soon before the next, as to prove, very likely, in the long run, more fatiguing than refreshing." Or the socks of the footsore Watt call for ceremonious attention:

> By wearing, on the foot that was too small, not one sock of his pair of socks, but both, and on the foot that was too large, not the other, but none, Watt strove in vain to correct this asymmetry. But logic was on his side, and he remained faithful, when involved in a journey of any length, to this distribution of his socks, in preference to the other three.

That there should be three other distributions of two socks, and that this, which has been chosen, can be resolved into its elements and reasons assigned thereto; that logic indeed is on the side of this one only: to linger in the presence of these truths yields to the pedantic mind enduring satisfaction, into which is appreciably subsumed the raw discomfort of wearing a boot, size twelve, and a shoe, size ten, on feet sized each eleven. So inventory yields ceremony, and ceremony anesthesia.

Quotation is a mode of ceremony. "What are those wonderful lines?" asks the buried Winnie time and again, calling to her aid scraps ne'er so well express'd: ". . . Go forget me why should something o'er that something shadow fling . . ." —small rituals of the sensibility, once learned, now from the ebbing memory summoned up for refingering. "One loses one's classics," she reflects with a sigh.

> Oh not all. (Pause.) A part. (Pause.) A part remains. (Pause.) That is what I find so wonderful, a part remains, of one's classics, to help one through the day.

By similar means as much of the given and actual as has lodged in the understanding can be decalcified. The real gives up its strangeness, the unexpected its arbitrariness, for the pedantic intellect that can perceive the unexpected event as a term in a series of events, and enumerate additional terms in that series, or that can accept the real thing as but the actualization of one potentiality among many, and consider in turn the others. So the absurdity of the arrangements by which the dog and the remains of Mr. Knott's food are brought together is alleviated, for Watt, by considering alternative arrangements as the author of these arrangements must have considered them, and discarding them as he must have discarded them. ("Not that for a moment Watt supposed that he had penetrated the forces at play, in this particular instance, or even perceived the forms that they upheaved, or obtained the least useful information concerning himself, or Mr Knott, for he did not. But he had turned, little by little, a disturbance into words, he had made a pillow of old words, for a head.")

So far are these passages, and the mental processes they enumerate, from idiosyncracy, that an Abelard would have gloried in them. They apotheosize the long labor of the West to restore the particular to its genera, and assign the genera to causes, and subsume causes in the First Cause, so pillowing many a head teased by among other things (we may speculate) the inherent ordonnance of the Latin language, which ought to be communicable to the obdurate things language handles. Scholastic philosophy could not have been carried on in, say, English prose as it stood in the thirteenth century. Modern English prose was developed in the seventeenth century to fill the need for a vernacular for such things as Latin speculation to be translated into. Beckett in the same way abandoned English after *Watt*, having carried as far as he could an English much indebted to the Ithaca episode of *Ulysses*, and conceived his trilogy with the assistance of French. He subsequently developed a new English in the course of translating what he had conceived in a different linguistic climate. He could hardly have done both jobs at once.

3

And here we encounter his concern with number. It is not that of a bookkeeper or a physicist; it sorts with the cadences of pedantry and allies itself with the Pythagorean and Augustinian pursuit of essences. The universe of number is not only one whose internal relationships are locked in place for the pedantic intellect to fondle in tranquility forever, it is also a world devoid of gritty specification. Its points have position without magnitude, its forms not only formal perfection but ideal non-existence. If they specify the mundane, it is by coincidence, as the fine six-place recurring decimal which Watt hears sung by an invisible choir—

Fifty two point two eight five seven one four two eight five seven one four two

—happens to reduce to decimal notation a leap year expressed in weeks. The song goes on to speak of blooming, withering, drooping, and the passage of generations; but these processes can be purged away and the longest year contemplated under an ideal aspect, climate abridged, pain negated, devouring Time blunting no lion's claws, by whoever knows how to divide 7 into 366. He will empty it also of lions, suns, and love, but no procedure is unflawed. "To know nothing is nothing," Molloy reflects, "not to want to know anything likewise, but to be beyond knowing anything, to know you are beyond knowing anything,[8] that is when peace enters in, to the soul of the incurious seeker.

---

[8] The French text is sharper: "Car ne rien savoir, ce n'est rien, ne rien vouloir savoir non plus, mais ne rien pouvoir savoir, savoir ne rien pouvoir savoir. . . ."

It is then the true division begins, of 22 by 7 for example, and the pages fill with the true ciphers at last." Twenty-two by 7 is the schoolbook approximation to pi, the circle-squarer. And the "true ciphers" are 3.142857, 142857, 142857 . . . , accumulating, to no definite end, invariable patterns that grow less and less significant. As their sum gradually approximates toward the secret of the circle, their importance gradually dwindles toward zero. They are also, oddly enough, the same figures that recur in the invisible choir's reduction of the year to weeks, as though Time itself were circular. "Why, Mr. Joyce seems to say, should there be four legs to a table," wrote Beckett twenty years before he conceived Molloy, "and four to a horse, and four seasons and four Gospels and four Provinces in Ireland? . . ."

Pi recalls Pythagoras and the dialogues with Duthuit. The art which, helpless, unable to come into being, does come into being ("Why?" "I don't know.") has a taste for the extreme case on which the very logic of the artist's situation converges. Beckett invariably backs the mode he is practicing into its last corner, and is most satisfied if he can render further performance in that mode, by him, impossible. Every game is an endgame. If fiction, for instance, mirrors the minutiae of life, then there stretches before every fiction-writer an infinity of possible novels: more various even, if that be possible, than life, since after a time the novels themselves commence to interbreed. But if the series can be made not to diverge but to converge toward some limit, then very close to that limit we shall find the Beckettian writer amassing his negligible increments. Fiction, for instance, will converge if narrator M_1 and his story are inventions of narrator M_2, who in turn . . . In Beckett's particular realization of this series the increments grow negligible after three terms, the third being called, with a nod at Pythagoras, The Unnamable. Its trailing off is documented in a series of thirteen Textes Pour Rien, the limit of the series being perhaps zero and the final words being

> que tout serait silencieux et vide et noir, comme maintenant, comme bientôt, quand tout sera fini, tout dit, dit-elle, murmure-t-elle.

This procedure has, not unsurprisingly, the shape of the classic statement of the classic Pythagorean problem. That aboriginal surd, the square root of two, which threw the custodians of the rational into panic, is exactly

$$1 + \cfrac{1}{2 + \cfrac{1}{2 + \cfrac{1}{2 + \cfrac{1}{2 + \dots}}}}$$

the denominator growing steadily emptier the further we carry it, and the expression as tidy to even the untrained eye as Beckett's converging fictions, even in abstract statement, are to the mind.

The analogy grows still tidier once we realize its range and simplicity, for surds and continued fractions are not the obstreperous rarities they may seem. Begin by imagining, tidily arrayed, all the numbers there are: the *domain of the rational numbers*—all the integers, all the fractions, stretching to infinity on either side of Zero: a domain vast, orderly, and accessible to anyone who can count pennies or cut a pie. Any member of this domain can be precisely located with respect to its neighbors (seven is midway between six and eight), precisely identified in terms of them (five is three plus two), precisely ranked with reference to them (fifteen is larger than seven and one-half, and is moreover just twice as large). Each has its name, its address, its normal occupation, like Remy de Gourmont's bourgeoisie ("animal reproducteur, animal électoral, animal contribuable"). On this plane move Micawber, Becky Sharp, Emma Bovary, Julien Sorel; also Pozzo and Moran.

But next imagine this domain shadowed and interpenetrated by the domain of the irrational numbers, infinitely more numerous, each maintaining its station in the unexpected gaps between adjacent rationals, which normally ignore its existence as the bourgeois ignores the *clochard*. These anomalies we can more or less locate, but not exactly; the best we can do is narrow down the limits between which they lurk. Thus between $1 \frac{2}{5}$ and $1 \frac{5}{12}$, or more exactly between $1 \frac{12}{29}$ and $1 \frac{29}{70}$, or more exactly still between $1 \frac{169}{408}$ and $1 \frac{70}{169}$ we may expect the root of two to exist, though we should not expect to find it. (Molloy, Moran thinks early in his quest, is somewhere "in the Molloy country," namely "that narrow region whose administrative limits he had never crossed.") Should we be able to find one, we could not, in the usual way, express it in terms of its neighbors, though without having found it we can give it a name. ("Molloy, or Mollose, was no stranger to me," recalls Moran. "Perhaps I had invented him, I mean found him ready made in my head.") Their existence, as the Pythagoreans perceived, is essentially scandalous, overturning as it does one's settled belief that the rational domain will suffice to contain all conceivable entities and all practical operations. ("If anyone else had spoken to me of Molloy I would have requested him to stop and I myself would not have confided his existence to a living soul for anything in the world.") If we are forced to name it more precisely, we can add terms to an endless decimal of which only the initial processes are accessible. ("What I heard, in my soul, I suppose, where the acoustics are so bad, was a first syllable, Mol, very clear, followed almost at once by a second, very thick, as though gobbled by the first, and which might have been oy as it might have been ose, or one, or even oc.") It exists, we know, between converging limits. "[Molloy] had very little room. His time too was limited. He hastened incessantly on, as if in despair, towards extremely close objectives. Now, a prisoner, he hurled himself at I know not what narrow confines, and now, hunted, he sought refuge near the centre.") We can also conceive of operations to be performed with such an unutterably entity, just as we can perform the standard arithmetical operations with a rational number once we have located it. ("My particular duties never terminated with the running to earth. That would have been too easy. But I had always to deal with the client in one way or another, according to instructions. Such operations took a multitude of forms, from the most vigorous to the most discreet.") Molloy, needless to say, is never found; for Moran ("so meticulous and calm in the main, so patiently turned towards the outer world as towards the lesser evil, . . . reining back his thoughts within the limits of the calculable") has been assigned a quest which to discharge he would have to forsake the rational domain where alone he can exist and try to conceive his quarry. He contemplates, composing himself for the quest, a domain "where masses move, stark as laws. Masses of what? One does not ask." Only in this atmosphere "of finality without end" can he venture to consider the work in hand. "For where Molloy could not be, nor Moran either for that matter, there Moran could bend over Molloy."

In this other domain which we can think about but not enter with our minds the irrational numbers exist, more numerous even than the infinitely numerous rationals. And it is in the analogy between these interpenetrating but incommensurable domains that Beckett discerns his central analogy for the artist's work and the human condition. ("There somewhere man is too, vast conglomerate of all of nature's kingdoms, as lonely and as bound.") As the Molloy domain is to the Moran, as that of the irrational numbers is to that of the rational, so the clown's is to the citizen's. The clown's role is a furtive enactment of all that orderly behavior will never attain to. He is sometimes wistful, more often in the Beckett landscape self-sufficient, always elusive, trapped between converging limits but never bound. The very shape of the Beckett plots, as Vivian Mercier has brilliantly noted,[9] can be prescribed by equations, Cartesian Man's inflexible oracles; Watt's career the curve of a function that approaches and turns around zero (Knott) before disappearing irretrievably off the paper, The Unnamable perhaps a spiral confined to the third quadrant where both coordinates are negative, and capable of straightening out and blending with zero if only it can protract itself to infinity.

The processes of mathematics offer themselves to the Beckett protagonists as a bridge into number's realm of the spectrally perfect, where enmired existence may be annihilated by essence utterly declared. Let a calculation get under way, let but a waft of mathematical terminology pass across the page, and the unpurged images of day recede. At least it is reasonable to expect that they will, but Beckett's is a world of anticlimax. It is a true that Arsene nearly succeeds in freezing gluttony into a formal composition with the merest touch of Euclidean symmetry:

---

9 "The Mathematical Limit," in *The Nation*, Feb. 14, 1959, 144.

> . . . At the moment that one hand presses, with open
> palm, between the indefatigable jaws, a cold potato,
> onion, tart, or sandwich, the other darts into the pouch
> and there, unerringly, fastens on a sandwich, onion, tart,
> or cold potato, as Mary wills. And the former, on its way
> down to be filled, meets the latter on its way up to be
> emptied, at a point equidistant from their points of
> departure, or arrival. . . .

But Molloy is not so lucky in his attempt to deal with the
frequent escapes of gas from his fundament. "It's hard not
to mention it now and then, however great my distaste.
One day I counted them." Struggling in vain to reduce
three hundred and fifteen occasions in nineteen hours to
some inconspicuous statistic, he subsides before the obduracy of "not even one fart every four minutes. It's un-
believable. Damn it, I hardly fart at all, I should never
have mentioned it. Extraordinary how mathematics help
you to know yourself." No consternation, however, can
unseat his grammatical punctilio, and "mathematics" gov-
erns a plural verb.

Sometimes it is the transition from data to numeration
that gives trouble, since the grip between these two worlds
must occur in an imperfectly prehensile mind. Having
been thrown down a flight of stairs, the protagonist of
"L'Expulsé" would welcome a talismanic figure to sustain
his contention that the flight was after all not a long one.
Alas, though he had counted them a thousand times,
"I have never known whether you should say one with your
foot on the sidewalk, two with the following foot on the
first step, and so on, or whether the sidewalk shouldn't
count. At the top of the steps I met with the same dilemma.
In the other direction, I mean from top to bottom, it was
the same, the word is not too strong. . . . I arrived therefore
at three totally different figures, without ever knowing which
of them was right." Worse yet, he remembers none of the

three, and all three are moreover essential; for to recall one, or two, of three adjacent numbers does not empower you to deduce the missing two, or one.

At least once a literal calculation (Lat. *calculus*, a stone used in reckoning) arouses the disinterested mania for symmetry, and proves as taxing to Molloy's limited talents as, no doubt, the half-developed calculus was to Newton's. He has sixteen stones, and four pockets; and without numbering the stones, he would insure that he can suck each one of them in turn, without risk, before the conclusion of the series, of sucking the same one twice. No more desperate assault on the randomness of things has ever been chronicled. He pounds his fists in rage, fills page after page with the narrative of strategies discarded, and settles at last for a Pyrrhic victory answering the conditions of the problem but marred by two aesthetic flaws. That is to say, the problem is only stunned, not solved at all, for it was an aesthetic problem from its inception. He has been compelled to sacrifice "the principle of trim," which would have kept the stones perpetually in uniform sets of four, and he has negotiated a short-term solution valid through any cycle of sixteen but never reliably repeatable. So the dream of commanding a method adequate to even the scanty requirements of sucking-stones is dissipated in compromise and frustration, and asceticism at length replaces system. He throws away all of the stones but one, and that one he ultimately loses.

Over the Beckett landscape, then, there hovers an inaccessible world of number and relation, to which his people fitfully try to approximate their actions. Molloy attempts circular movement, but achieves perhaps a great polygon ("perfection is not of this world."). One of The Unnamable's surrogates moves in spirals. Murphy considers with agitation that his assortment of five biscuits will not "spring to life before him, dancing the radiant measure of its total permutability, edible in a hundred and twenty ways!" until he can learn not to prefer any one to any other. His preference for the Ginger, which he saves for the last, leaves only four to permute in twenty-four ways; and his distaste for the Anonymous biscuit, which he therefore wolfs immediately, further reduces the number of ways in which he can consume the remainder to "a paltry six," his egregious selfhood diminishing the spectrum of availability twentyfold. Utter ablation of choice will confer utter freedom, which is by definition access to some plane on which all possibilities are equally available because all have been cleansed of identity and significance: and this is the world of number: "Neither elements nor states, nothing but forms becoming and crumbling into the fragments of a new becoming, without love or hate or any intelligible principle of change." Here Murphy (if he can enter this world, which he bears somewhere within him) is position without magnitude, "a point in the ceaseless unconditioned generation and passing away of line." (If Sisyphus thinks each journey is the first, thinks Moran, that "would keep hope alive would it not, hellish hope. Whereas to see yourself doing the same thing endlessly over and over again fills you with satisfaction.")

To consider, with Murphy that bliss consists of the full availability of all the elements of a set that are theoretically possible, is to encounter from a new direction the unique translucent enumerating style, which educes from whatever it handles the delights of total co-presence, nothing abridged. It works by a tireless survey of possibilities, rotating each being and situation before the mind in an arctic clarity of disclosure.

All three take off their hats simultaneously, press their hands to their foreheads, concentrate.

ESTRAGON: (*triumphantly*). Ah!

VLADIMIR: He has it.

POZZO: (*impatient*). Well?

ESTRAGON: Why doesn't he put down his bags?

VLADIMIR: Rubbish!

POZZO: Are you sure?

VLADIMIR: Damn it haven't you already told us?

POZZO: I've already told you?

ESTRAGON: He's already told us?

VLADIMIR: Anyway he has put them down.

ESTRAGON: (*glance at Lucky*). So he has. And what of it?

VLADIMIR: Since he has put down his bags it is impossible we should have asked why he does not do so.

POZZO: Stoutly reasoned!

ESTRAGON: And why has he put them down?

POZZO: Answer us that.

VLADIMIR: In order to dance.

ESTRAGON: True!

POZZO: True!

Silence. They put on their hats.

"Haven't you already told us?" "I've already told you?" "He's already told us?" This is worthy of Bach. It is a dramatic extreme of the style which in its lyric extreme generates the indefatigable enumerations, in *Watt*, of every relevant qualifying circumstance.

Well, said Mr Fitzwein, it is always a pleasure for us, for me for one for my part, and for my colleagues for two for theirs, to meet a moron from a different crawl of life from our crawl, from my crawl and from their crawl. And to that extent I suppose we are obliged to you, Mr Louit. But I do not think we grasp, I do not think that I grasp and I should be greatly surprised to learn that my collaborators grasp, what this gentleman has to do with the object of your recent visit, Mr Louit, your recent brief and, if you will allow me to say so, prodigal visit to the western seaboard.

Like a circle straining to approach or recede from its center, this discourse is held between prodigality and ellipsis by opposed forces that ensure its elegant curve, ceremonious but never diffuse. Like the planets in their courses it discloses as it makes its way the laws which appear to be governing its movement, but which in fact serve only as a summary description. There is not an obscure instant; the syntax combs out and distinguishes thousands of short words, syntactic permutations keep them in motion, and repeatedly the precise individual word ("crawl," "moron," "prodigal,") reminds us that this elegance is not hypnotized by its own formulae, that its eyes are constantly open. It is an austere prose, not narcissistic nor baroque. It is not opulent. It moves with the great calm of some computation, doing a thousand things but only necessary ones. Such is the aesthetic of *Watt*, where the style declares itself fully.

In subsequent works it complicates itself. It seizes on smaller systems and permutes their elements more rapidly, producing a less ample surface, a more rapid rate of involution. But to the last syllable of *Comment C'est* it works by enumeration and permutation, longing to be threading Murphy's delicious world of darkness where all combinations are equally available. Here is Moran trying out a newly stiffened knee:

> . . . But when you sit down on the ground you must sit down tailor-wise, or like a foetus, these are so to speak the only possible positions, for a beginner. So that I was not long in letting myself fall back flat on my back. And I was not long either in making the following addition to the sum of my knowledge, that when of the innumerable attitudes adopted unthinkingly by the normal man all are precluded but two or three, then these are enhanced. . . . And it would not surprise me if the great classic paralyses were to offer analogous and perhaps

even still more unspeakable satisfactions. To be literally incapable of motion at last, that must be something! My mind swoons when I think of it. And mute into the bargain! And perhaps deaf as a post! And who knows blind as a bat! And as likely as not your memory a blank! And just enough brain intact to allow you to exult! And to dread death like a regeneration.

From savoring the sensations of a stiff knee to coveting the great classic paralyses, there is no flaw in this logic. It is not by chance that within a page Moran has begun to contemplate shoring up his decaying body with a bicycle: the machine, wrote Jack B. Yeats, that runs by the power of arithmetic.

The Cartesian Centaur

. . . whilst this machine is to him. . .
— *Hamlet*

Il n'y a plus de roues de bicyclette.
—*Fin de Partie*

Molloy had a bicycle, Moran was carried on the luggage rack of a bicycle, Malone recalls the cap of the bell of a bicycle, bicycles pass before Watt's eyes at the beginning and at the end of his transit through the house of Knott; Clov begged for a bicycle while bicycles still existed, and while there were still bicycles it was the wreck of a tandem that deprived Nagg and Nell of their legs. Like the bowler hat and the letter M, the bicycle makes at irregular intervals a silent transit across the Beckett *paysage intérieur,* whether to convince us that this place has after all an identity of sorts, or else like the poet's jar in Tennessee to supply for a while some point about which impressions may group themselves. If it is never a shiny new substantial bicycle, always a bicycle lost, a bicycle remembered, like Nagg's legs or Molloy's health, that is a circumstance essential to its role; like the body it disintegrates, like the body's vigor it retires into the past: *Hoc est enim corpus suum,* an ambulant frame, in Newtonian equilibrium.

Molloy is separated from his bicycle as the first stage in a disintegration which entails the stiffening of one leg, the shortening of the other leg which had previously been stiff, the loss of the toes from one foot (he forgets which), a staggering in circles, a crawling, a dragging of

117

himself flat on his belly using his crutches like grapnels, brief thoughts of rolling, and final immobility, in a ditch. "Molloy could stay, where he happened to be." Formerly, while he possessed the bicycle, he had a less derelict posture in which to stay where he happened to be:

> Every hundred yards or so I stopped to rest my legs, the good one as well as the bad, and not only my legs, not only my legs. I didn't properly speaking get down off the machine, I remained astride it, my feet on the ground, my arms on the handle-bars, and I waited until I felt better.

In this tableau man and machine mingle in conjoint stasis, each indispensable to the other's support. At rest, the bicycle extends and stabilizes Molloy's endoskeleton. In motion, too, it complements and amends his structural deficiencies:

> I was no mean cyclist, at that period. This is how I went about it. I fastened my crutches to the cross-bar, one on either side, I propped the foot of my stiff leg (I forget which, now they're both stiff) on the projecting front axle, and I pedalled with the other. It was a chainless bicycle, with a free-wheel, if such a bicycle exists. Dear bicycle, I shall not call you bike, you were green, like so many of your generation, I don't know why. . . .

This odd machine exactly complements Molloy. It even compensates for his inability to sit down ("the sitting posture was not for me any more, because of my short stiff leg"); and it transfers to an ideal, Newtonian plane of rotary progression and gyroscopic stability those locomotive expedients improbably complex for the intact human being, and for the crippled Molloy impossible.

In various passages of the canon, Beckett has gone into these expedients in some detail. For more than half a page he enumerates the several classes of local movement entailed by "Watt's way of advancing due east, for example";

the protagonist of "L'Expulsé" devotes some 500 words to a similar topic, noting that every attempt to modify his somewhat awkward methods "always ended in the same way, I mean by a loss of equilibrium, followed by a fall," while the characteristic progression of the protagonist of "Le Calmant" "seemed at every step to solve a statodynamic problem without precedent." "The hands and knees, love, try the hands and knees," cries Winnie in *Happy Days*. "The knees! The knees! (*Pause*.) What a curse, mobility." For the human body is to the Newtonian understanding an intolerably defective machine. It possesses, in the upright position, no equilibrium whatever; only by innumerable little compensatory shiftings does it sustain the illusion that it is standing motionless, and when it moves forward on its legs it does so by periodic surrender and recovery of balance, in a manner too hopelessly immersed in the *ad hoc* for analytic reconstruction. Every step is improvised, except by such dogged systematizers as Watt. And this was the kind of machine whose union with the pure intelligence puzzled Descartes, who invented the mode of speculation in which all Beckett's personages specialize.

> But there is nothing which that nature teaches me more expressly than that I have a body which is ill affected when I feel pain, and stands in need of food and drink when I experience the sensations of hunger and thirst, etc. And therefore I ought not to doubt but that there is some truth in these informations.

That last sentence, despite Descartes' proclaimed certainty, has Molloy's tone, and the whole passage—it is from the Sixth Meditation (1641)—prompts comparison with certain speculations of The Unnamable:

> . . . Equate me, without pity or scruple, with him who exists, somehow, no matter how, no finicking, with him whose story this story had the brief ambition to be. Bet-

ter, ascribe to me a body. Better still, arrogate to me a mind. Speak of a world of my own, sometimes referred to as the inner, without choking. Doubt no more. Seek no more. Take advantage of the brand-new substantiality to abandon, with the only possible abandon, deep down within. And finally, these and other decisions having been taken, carry on cheerfully as before. Something has changed nevertheless.

These fiats and revulsions come closer to the Cartesian spirit than Descartes himself; for Descartes, when he took his attention away from the immutable truths of mathematics, could resolve manifold confusions about the human estate "on the ground alone that God is no deceiver, and that consequently he has permitted no falsity in my opinions which he has not likewise given me a faculty of correcting." But this premise comes from outside the System, and a Molloy or a Malone have little confidence in it; to say nothing of The Unnamable, who assumes that the superior powers deceive continually. The Beckett protagonists would accord the classic resolutions of the Cartesian doubt a less apodictic weight than Descartes does; and notably his conclusion that the body, "a machine made by the hands of God," is "incomparably better arranged, and adequate to movements more admirable than is any machine of human invention." For unlike that of Molloy, the Cartesian body seems not subject to loss of toes or arthritis of the wrists.

So committed is Descartes to this perfect corporeal mechanism, that the question how a fine machine might be told from a man requires his most careful attention, especially in view of the circumstance that a machine can do almost anything better: "A clock composed only of wheels and weights can number the hours and measure time more exactly than we with all our skill." His answer is far from rigorous, based as it is on just that interpenetration of body and reason which he is elsewhere so hard put to explain. Molloy or Malone would have less difficulty with this question. The body, if we consider it without prejudice in the light of the seventeenth-century connoisseurship of the simple machines, is distinguished from any machine, however complex, by being clumsy, sloppy, and unintelligible; the extreme of analytic ingenuity will resolve no one of its functions, except inexactly, into lever, wedge, wheel, pulley, screw, inclined plane, or some combination of these. If we would admire a body worthy of the human reason, we shall have to create it, as the Greeks did when they united the noblest functions of rational and animal being, man with horse, and created the breed to which they assigned Chiron, tutor of Asclepius, Jason, and Achilles. For many years, however, we have had accessible to us a nobler image of bodily perfection than the horse. The Cartesian Centaur is a man riding a bicycle, *mens sana in corpore disposito.*

This being rises clear of the muddle in which Descartes leaves the mind-body relationship. The intelligence guides, the mobile wonder obeys, and there is no mysterious interpenetration of function. (The bicycle, to be sure, imposes conditions; there is no use in the intelligence attemptng to guide it up a tree. God in the same way cannot contradict His own nature.) Down a dead street, in "Le Calmant," passes at an unassignable time a phantom cyclist, all the while reading a paper which with two hands he holds unfolded before his eyes. So body and mind go each one nobly about its business, without interference or interaction. From time to time he rings his bell, without ceasing to read, until optical laws of unswerving precision have reduced him to a point on the horizon. Across the entire Beckett landscape there passes no more self-sufficient image of felicity.

It grows clear why for Molloy to describe his bicycle at length would be a pleasure, and why Moran "would gladly write four thousand words" on the bicycle his son buys, which must once have been quite a good one. Though neither of these descriptions is ever written, we do receive a sufficiently technical account of the mode of union— not to say symbiosis—between each of these bicycles and its rider. ("Here then in a few words is the solution I arrived at. First the bags, then my son's raincoat folded in four, all lashed to the carrier and the saddle with my son's bits of string. As for the umbrella, I hooked it round my neck, so as to have both hands free to hold on to my son by the waist, under the armpits rather, for by this time my seat was higher than his. Pedal, I said. He made a despairing effort. I can well believe it. We fell. I felt a sharp pain in my shin. It was all tangled up in the back wheel. Help! I cried. . . .") The world is an imperfect place; this theme deserves to be explicated on a more ideal plane. Let us try.

Consider the cyclist as he passes, the supreme specialist, transfiguring that act of moving from place to place which is itself the sentient body's supreme specialty. He is the term of locomotive evolution from slugs and creeping things. Could Gulliver have seen this phenomenon he would have turned aside from the Houyhnhnms, and Plato have reconsidered the possibility of incarnating an idea. Here all rationalist metaphysics terminates (as he pedals by, reciprocating motion steadily converted into rotary). The combination is impervious to Freud, and would have been of no evident use to Shakespeare. This glorified body is the supreme Cartesian achievement, a product of the pure intelligence, which has preceded it in time and now dominates it in function. It is neither generated nor (with reasonable care) corrupted. Here Euclid achieves mobility: circle, triangle, rhombus, the clear and distinct patterns of Cartesian knowledge. Here gyroscopic stability vies for attention with the ancient paradox of the still point and the rim. (He pedals with impenetrable dignity, the sitting posture combined with the walking, *sedendo et ambulando*, philosopher-king.) To consider the endless perfection of the chain, the links forever settling about the cogs, is a perpetual pleasure; to reflect that a specified link is alternately stationary with respect to the sprocket, then in motion with respect to the same sprocket, without hiatus between these conditions, is to entertain the sort of soothing mystery which, as Moran remarked "with rapture" in another connection, you can study all your life and never understand. The wheels are a miracle; the contraption moves on air, sustained by a network of wires in tension not against gravity but against one another. The Litany of the Simple Machines attends his progress. *Lever, Pulley, Wheel and Axle*: the cranks, the chain, the wheels. *Screw*, the coaster brake. *Wedge*, the collar that attends to the security of the handlebars. And the climax is of transparent subtlety, for owing to the inclination of the front fork, the bicycle, if its front wheel veers left or right, is returned to a straight course by the action of an invisible sixth simple machine, the *Inclined Plane*; since so long as it is not holding a true course it is troubled by the conviction that it is trying to run up hill, and this it prefers not to do. Here is the fixation of childhood dream, here is the fulfillment of young manhood. All human faculties are called into play, and all human muscles except perhaps the auricular. Thus is fulfilled the serpent's promise to Eve, *et eritis sicut dii*; and it is right that there should ride about France as these words are written, subject to Mr. Beckett's intermittent attention, a veteran racing cyclist, bald, a "stayer," recurrent placeman in town-to-town and national championships, Christian name elusive, surname Godeau, pronounced, of course, no differently from Godot.[1]

Monsieur Godeau, it is clear from our speculations, typifies Cartesian Man in excelsis, the Cartesian Centaur, body and mind in close harmony: the mind set on survival, mastery, and the contemplation of immutable relativities (*tout passe, et tout dure*), the body a reduction to uncluttered terms of the quintessential machine. From the Beckett canon it is equally clear that M. Godot, this solving and transforming paragon, does not come today, but perhaps tomorrow, and that meanwhile the Molloys, Morans, and Malones of this world must shift as they can, which is to say, badly. Cartesian man deprived of his bicycle is a mere intelligence fastened to a dying animal.

The dying animal preserves, however, stigmata of its higher estate. Molloy, after his bicycle has been abandoned, does not then resign himself to the human shuffle and forego that realm where arc, tangent, and trajectory describe the locus of ideal motion. No, even in his uncycled state he is half mechanized; he can lever himself forward, "swinging slowly through the sullen air."

> There is rapture, or there should be, in the motion crutches give. It is a series of little flights, skimming the ground. You take off, you land, through the thronging sound in wind and limb, who have to fasten one foot on the ground before they dare lift up the other. And even their most joyous hastening is less aerial than my hobble.

---

[1] It may calm the skeptical reader to know that my knowledge of this man comes from Mr. Beckett.

("But these are reasonings, based on analysis," he is careful to add, locating but not submitting to the tragic flaw in the Cartesian paradise.) After his legs give out he is able to adapt the principle of the rack and pawl: "Flat on my belly, using my crutches like grapnels, I plunged them ahead of me into the undergrowth, and when I felt they had a hold, I pulled myself forward, with an effort of the wrists." Periodically, as he crashes forward in this way, like the prototype of a moon-camion, he improves on the analogy with a bicycle of some inefficient pattern by blowing his horn ("I had taken it off my bicycle") through the cloth of his pocket. "Its hoot was fainter every time."

Reciprocating motion, it seems, is a characteristic of Molloy's, whether mounted on his bicycle or not. The unusual chainless bicycle, transmitting power apparently locomotive-fashion by the reciprocating rod,[2] accents this motif. Nor is he the only person in these books whose mode of progression is a studied and analyzed thing, distinct from human inconsequence. It is oddly relevant to say of Beckett characters, as of Newtonian bodies, that they are either at rest or in motion; and in the Beckett universe, motion, for those who are capable of setting themselves in motion, is an enterprise meriting at least a detailed description, and more likely prolonged deliberation. Malone's creature Macmann, for example, commences to roll on the ground, and finds himself "advancing with regularity, and even a certain rapidity, along the arc of a gigantic circle probably," one of his extremities being heavier than the other "but not by much." "And without reducing his speed he began to dream of a flat land where he would never have to rise again and

---

[2] Mr. Beckett recalls seeing such a bicycle when he was a boy in Dublin.

hold himself erect in equilibrium, first on the right foot for example, then on the left, and where he might come and go and so survive after the fashion of a great cylinder endowed with the faculties of cognition and volition."

Malone himself, on the other hand, is at rest; and so far is the Cartesian mechanism dismantled, that it would take, he estimates, several weeks to re-establish connection between his brain and his feet, should there be any need for that. He has, needless to say, no bicycle, and nowhere speaks of a bicycle; but he includes among his possessions not only half a crutch but the cap of his bicycle bell: the least rudiment, like the knucklebone of a dinosaur. Yet to him too occurs the idea of playing at Prime Mover: "I wonder if I could not contrive, wielding my stick like a punt-pole, to move my bed. It may well be on castors, many beds are. Incredible I should never have thought of this, all the time I have been here. I might even succeed in steering it, it is so narrow, through the door, and even down the stairs, if there is a stairs that goes down." Unhappily at the first trial he loses hold of the stick instead, and meditating on this disaster claims intellectual kinship with another speculative Mover: "I must have missed my point of purchase in the dark. Sine qua non. Archimedes was right."

Let Archimedes' presence disconcert no one: the Beckett bicycle can orchestrate all the great themes of human speculation. Since the Beckett people transact their most palpable business in some universe of absence, however, it is without surprise that we discover the bicycle to have put in its most extended and paradigmatic appearance in a novel which has not been published. This is the composition of *c.* 1945 which details certain advantures of what The Unnamable is later to call "the pseudocouple Mercier-Camier." I translate from a French typescript:

You remember our bicycle? said Mercier.

Yes, said Camier.

Speak up, said Mercier. I hear nothing.

I remember our bicycle, said Camier.

There remains of it, solidly chained to a railing, said Mercier, that which can reasonably be said to remain, after more than eight days' incessant rain, of a bicycle from which have been subtracted the two wheels, the saddle, the bell, and the carrier. And the reflector, he added. I nearly forgot that. What a head I have.

And the pump, naturally, said Camier.

You may believe me or you may not, said Mercier, it is all the same to me, but they have left us our pump.

Yet it was a good one, said Camier. Where is it?

I suppose it was simply overlooked in error, said Mercier. So I left it there. It seemed the most reasonable course. What have we to pump up, at present? In fact I inverted it. I don't know why. Something compelled me.

It stays just as well inverted? said Camier.

Oh, quite as well, said Mercier.

This exchange bristles with problems. Having undergone a Molloy's dismemberment, has the bicycle at some stage rendered up its identity? Or is it identifiable only as one identifies a corpse? And in no other way? In some other way? Again, assuming that a bisected rhomboid frame of steel tubing equipped with handlebars and a sprocket is recognizably a bicycle, has this congeries of sensible appearances relinquished its essence with the removal of the wheels? From its two wheels it is named, on its two wheels it performs its essential function. To what extent ought a decisiveness of nomenclature persuade us to equate function, essence, and identity? These are matters to agitate a schoolman; they would certainly have engaged the careful attention of Watt. Mercier, *homme moyen sensuel,* is sufficiently schooled in precision to acknowledge in passing the problem, what can reasonably be said to remain of a bicycle thus reduced, but insufficiently curious to pursue this investigation. His attention lingers instead, a bit antiseptically, on two human problems, the first perhaps ethical (whether, since the anonymous autopsist has presumably only forgotten the pump, it ought not to be left for him) and the second hermeneutic (why, having chosen to leave it, he himself did not forbear to turn it upside down).

These several classes of questions, as it turns out, are of greater formal brilliance than practical import. The Mercier-Camier universe is soured by unassignable final causes, as in their astringent laconism the two of them seem half to acknowledge. They are in the presence, actually, of an archetypal event, or perhaps a portent, or perhaps a cause: there is no telling. In retrospect, anyhow, one thing is clear: from the dismemberment of their bicycle we may date the disintegration of Mercier and Camier's original lock-step unity. In the final third of this novel they gradually become nodding acquaintances, like the two wheels which were once sustained by a single frame but are now free to pursue independent careers. This separation is not willed, it simply occurs, like the dissolution of some random conjunction of planets: "pseudo-couple," indeed.

For The Unnamable there is no stick, no Archimedes, no problem whatever of the Malone order, or of the Mercier-Camier order, chiefly because there is no verifiable body; and there is no mention of a bicycle nor reflection of a bicycle nor allusion to a bicycle from beginning to end of a novel, in this respect as in others, unprecedented in the Beckett canon. Nor is this unexpected; for *The Unnamable* is the final phase of a trilogy which carries the Cartesian process backwards, beginning with a bodily *je suis* and ending with a bare *cogito*. This reduction begins with a journey (Molloy's) and a dismembering of the Cartesian Centaur; its middle term (*Malone Dies*) is a stasis, dominated by the unallayable brain; and the third phase has neither the identity of rest nor that of motion, functions under the sign neither of matter nor of mind because it evades both, and concerns itself endlessly to no end with a baffling intimacy between discourse and non-existence.

This is not to say, however, that the fundamental problems of a seventeenth-century philosopher, and notably the problems of bodies in motion, do not confront The Unnamable in their baldest form. The first body in motion is, unexpectedly, Malone, appearing and disappearing "with the punctuality of clockwork, always at the same remove, the same velocity, in the same direction, the same attitude." He may be seated, he "wheels" without a sound; the evidence in fact points to his being borne through this ideal space on some quintessential bicycle. So much for cosmology. We next confront a certain Mahood, under two aspects: Mahood in motion, Mahood at rest. In motion, on crutches but minus a leg, he executes a converging spiral; at rest, he inhabits a jar. In either aspect, he is a Descartes cursed by the dark of the moon. At rest in the jar, he pursues the *cogito* sufficiently to think of demanding proof that he exists ("How all becomes clear and simple when one opens an eye on the within, having of course previously exposed it to the without, in order to benefit by the contrast."). So pursuing "the bliss of what is clear and simple," he pauses "to make a distinction (I must be still thinking):"

> That the jar is really standing where they say, all right, I wouldn't dream of denying it, after all it's none of my business, though its presence at such a place, about the reality of which I do not propose to quibble either, does

not strike me as very credible. No, I merely doubt that I am in it. It is easier to raise the shrine than bring the deity down to haunt it. . . . That's what comes of distinctions.

The jar, clearly, is what the body, geometrically conceived, is reducible to by the systematizing intelligence. As for the one-legged man with the crutch, he pursues his converging spiral (the first curve to have been rectified by Descartes), complementing with his ideally incommoded motion the other's ideally perplexed cogitation, and so completing a little cosmos pervaded by the two Cartesian functions, movement and thought. He jerks, hops, swings and falls, so remote from the ancient symbiosis with a bicycle as not even to be visited by such a possibility, yet enacting as best the deficiencies of the flesh will allow his intent parody of some obsessed machine. Molloy too progressed in spirals, "through imperfect navigation," and when he was in the woods slyly resolved to outwit the deception which is reputed to draw benighted travelers into involuntary circles: "Every three or four jerks I altered course, which permitted me to describe, if not a circle, at least a great polygon, perfection is not of this world, and to hope that I was going forward in a straight line." Molloy's is plane geometry; the spiral described by the surrogate of The Unnamable is located on the surface of a sphere, and hence, if it originates from a point, can enlarge itself only until it has executed a swing equal to the globe's greatest circumference, and after that must necessarily commence to close in again. When we take up his tale, his global sweep is converging into a very small space indeed, preliminary to the moment when it will have nothing to do but reverse itself for lack of room. At the pole of convergence we are surprised to discover his family, keeping watch, cheering him on ("Stick it, lad, it's your last winter."), singing hymns, recalling that he was a fine baby.

Yet none of the enmired but recognizably human will to prevail that once animated Molloy's progress toward his mother impresses the reader of these later pages. The narrative, for one thing, is no longer impregnated by indefatigable first person energy. Mahood's progress, half something experienced by The Unnamable but half something unreliably told him, is unhitched from his empathic passions, and endeavoring to recall his (or Mahood's) thoughts and feelings he can only report absorption in the technicalities of spiral progression. "The only problem for me was how to continue, since I could not do otherwise, to the best of my declining powers, in the motion which had been imparted to me." The annihilation of his family by poison does not arrest him as he completes his rounds, "stamping under foot the unrecognizable remains of my family, here a face, there a stomach, as the case might be, and sinking into them with the ends of my crutches both coming and going."

The bicycle is long gone, the Centaur dismembered; of the exhilaration of the cyclist's progress in the days when he was lord of the things that move, nothing remains but the ineradicable habit of persisting like a machine. The serene confidence of the lordly *Cogito* . . . is similarly dissociated, in this last phase of the dream of Cartesian man, into a garrulity, vestigially logical, which is perhaps piped into him by other beings: a condition oddly prefigured by the parrot which a friend of Malone's had tried to teach to enunciate the *Nihil in intellectu quod non prius in sensu*, a doctrine it would have travestied whenever it opened its beak. It got no further than *Nihil in intellectu*, followed by a series of squawks. More profoundly than its great forerunner, *Bouvard et*

Pécuchet, the Beckett trilogy takes stock of the Enlightenment, and reduces to essential terms the three centuries during which those ambitious processes of which Descartes is the symbol and progenitor (or was he too, like The Unnamable, spoken through by a Committee of the *Zeitgeist?*) accomplished the dehumanization of man. It is plain why Godot does not come. The Cartesian Centaur was a seventeenth-century dream, the fatal dream of being, knowing, and moving like a god. In the twentieth century he and his machine are gone, and only a desperate élan remains: "I don't know, I'll never know, in the silence you don't know, you must go on, I can't go on, I'll go on."

Life In The Box

"Once a certain degree of insight has been reached," said
Wylie, "all men talk, when talk they must, the same tripe."
—*Murphy*

1

The drama is a ritual enacted in an enclosed space into
which fifty or more people are staring. They are all more
or less patiently waiting for something: the Reversal, the
Discovery, the *Deus ex Machina,* or even the final curtain.
Settled numbly for the evening, they accept whatever interim diversions the stage can provide: tramps in bowler
hats, for instance.

The space into which they are staring is characterized
in some way: for instance, *A country road. A tree. Evening.*
"Evening" means that the illumination on stage is not
much brighter than in the auditorium. "A country road"
means that there is no set to look at. As for the tree, an
apologetic thing tentatively identified as a leafless weeping willow, it serves chiefly to denote the spot, like the
intersection (coordinates O,O) of the Cartesian axes.
"You're sure it was here?" "What?" "That we were to
wait." "He said by the tree." If it accretes meaning of an
anomalous sort in the course of the evening, reminding
us, when the two tramps stand beneath it with a rope,
of ampler beams which once suspended the Savior and
two thieves, or again of the fatal tree in Eden (and the
garden has, sure enough, vanished), or even of the
flowering staff in *Tannhäuser,* it does this not by being

133

explicated but simply by its insistent continual presence, during which, as adjacent events diffract the bleak light, we begin to entertain mild hallucinations about it. Only in a theater can we be made to look at a mock tree for that length of time. Drama is distinguished from all other forms of art by its control over the *time* spent by the spectator in the presence of its significant elements.

These events, these elements, assert only their own nagging existence. "The theatrical character," remarked Alain Robbe-Grillet in this connection, "*is on stage*, this is his primary quality—he is there." Hence, "the essential function of the theatrical performance: to show what this fact of *being there* consists of." Or as Beckett was later to write of a later play, "Hamm as stated, and Clov as stated, together as stated, *nec tecum nec sine te,* in such a place, and in such a world, that's all I can manage, more than I could."

In *Waiting for Godot,* the place with its tree is stated, together with a single actor engaged in a mime with his boot. His inability to get it off is the referent of his first words, "Nothing to be done," a sentence generally reserved for more portentous matters. To him enter the second actor, as in the medial phase of Greek Theater, and their talk commences. What they talk about first is the fact that they are both there, the one fact that is demonstrably true not only in art's agreed world but before our eyes. It is even the one certainty that survives an evening's waiting:

> BOY: What am I to tell Mr. Godot, sir?
> VLADIMIR: Tell him . . . (*he hesitates*) . . . tell him you saw us. (*Pause*) You did see us, didn't you?
> BOY: Yes Sir.

The realities stated with such insistence are disquietingly provisional. The tree is plainly a sham, and the two tramps are simply filling up time until a proper dramatic entertainment can get under way. They are helping the management fulfill, in a minimal way, its contract with the ticket holders. The resources of vaudeville are at their somewhat incompetent disposal: bashed hats, dropped pants, tight boots, the kick, the pratfall, the improper story. It will suffice if they can stave off a mass exodus until Godot comes, in whom we are all so interested. Beckett, it is clear, has cunningly doubled his play with that absence of a play which every confirmed theatergoer has at some time or other experienced, the advertized cynosure having missed a train or overslept or indulged in temperament. The tramps have plainly not learned parts; they repeatedly discuss what to do next ("What about hanging ourselves?") and observe from time to time that tedium is accumulating:

> Charming evening we're having.
> Unforgettable.
> And it's not over.
> Apparently not.
> It's only beginning.
> It's awful.
> Worse than the pantomime.
> The circus.
> The music-hall.
> The circus.

Thus a non-play comments on itself. Or the audience of the non-play is reminded that others the previous night sat in these seats witnessing the identical futility ("What did we do yesterday?" "In my opinion we were here.") and that others in turn will sit there watching on successive nights for an indeterminate period.

> We'll come back to-morrow [says tramp No. 1].
> And then the day after to-morrow.
> Possibly.
> And so on.

And so on, until the run of the production ends. It will end, presumably, when there are no longer spectators interested, though it is difficult to explain on Shakespearean premises what it is that they can be expected to be interested in. Or perhaps not so difficult. What brings the groundlings to *Macbeth*? Why, they are waiting for the severed head. And to *Hamlet*? They are waiting for Garrick (or Irving, or Olivier). And here?

> Let's go.
> We can't.
> Why not?
> We're waiting for Godot.
> (*despairingly*) Ah!

The French text manages an inclusiveness denied to English idiom: "Pourquoi?" "On attend Godot." Not *"nous"* but *"on"*: Didi, Gogo, and audience alike.

If the seeming improvisation of the tramps denies theatricality, it affirms at the same time quintessential theater, postulating nothing but what we can see on stage: a place, and men present in it, doing what they are doing. And into this quintessential theater there irrupts before long the strident unreality we crave:

> POZZO: (*terrifying voice*). I am Pozzo! (*Silence.*) Pozzo!
> (*Silence.*) Does that name mean nothing to you? (*Silence.*) I say does that name mean nothing to you?

This is at last the veritable stuff, that for which we paid our admissions: an actor, patently, with gestures and grimaces, who has furthermore memorized and rehearsed his part and knows how they talk in plays. He makes his entrance like Tamburlaine driving the pampered jades of Asia (represented, in this low-budget production, by one extra); he takes pains with his elocution, assisted by a vaporizer, like an effete *Heldentenor*; he recites a well-conned set speech on the twilight, with "vibrant," "lyrical," and "prosaic" phases, and contrapuntal assistance from well-schooled hands (two hands lapsing; two hands flung amply apart; one hand raised in admonition; fingers snapped at the climax, to reinforce the word "pop!"). This is theater; the evening is saved. Surely he is Godot?

But he says not; and we are disconcerted to find him fishing for applause, and from the tramps. They are his audience as we are his and theirs. The play, in familiar Beckett fashion, has gotten inside the play. So too when Lucky (who has also memorized his part) recites his set speech on the descent of human certainty into "the great cold the great dark" ("for reasons unknown but time will tell"), it is for the amusement of his master, and of the tramps, and incidentally of ourselves. The same is true of his symbolic dance, a thing of constrained gestures, as in Noh drama[1]. So the perspective continues to diminish, box within box. In this theater, the tramps. Within their futile world, the finished theatricality of Pozzo. At Pozzo's command, Lucky's speech; within this speech, scholarship, man *in posse* and *in esse*, all that which, officially endorsed, we think we know, notably the labors of the Acacacademy of Anthropopopometry; within these in turn, caca (Fr. colloq., excrement) and popo, a chamberpot: a diminution, a delirium.

Such metaphysics as the Beckett theater will permit is entailed in this hierarchy of watchers and watched. Throughout, and notably during Lucky's holocaust of phrases, we clutch at straws of meaning, persuaded at

---

1 "Do you know what he calls it? . . . The Net. He thinks he is entangled in a net." Compare the words Miscio Ito spoke, "with perfect precision," to Ezra Pound: "Japanese dance all time overcoat." The one stable item of Noh décor is painted on the back of the stage: "a pine tree, symbol of the unchanging."

bottom only of one thing, that all four men exist, embodied, gravid, speaking; moving before us, their shadows cast on the wall, their voices echoing in the auditorium, their feet heavy on the boards.

The second act opens with the song about the dog's epitaph, another infinitely converging series of acts and agents. The Unnamable also meditates on this jingle, and discovers its principle: "third verse, as the first, fourth, as the second, fifth, as the third, give us time, give us time and we'll be a multitude"; for it generates an infinite series of unreal beings, epitaph within epitaph within epitaph. Correspondingly, near the end of the act Didi muses over the sleeping Gogo:

> At me too someone is looking, of me too someone is saying, He is sleeping, he knows nothing, let him sleep on.

So we watch Didi move through his part, as he watches Gogo, and meanwhile Lucky's God with the white beard, outside time, without extension, is loving us dearly "with some exceptions for reasons unknown but time will tell."

It remains to recall that the Beckett universe, wherever we encounter it, consists of a shambles of phenomena within which certain symmetries and recurrences are observable, like the physical world as interpreted by early man. So this stage world has its structure and landmarks. We observe, for example, that bowler hats are apparently *de rigueur*, and that they are removed for thinking but replaced for speaking. We observe that moonrise and sunset occur in conjunction two nights running, for this is an ideal cosmology, unless we are to suppose the two acts to be separated by an interval of twenty-nine days. The tree by the same token has budded overnight, like an early miracle. All this is arbitrary because theatrical. Our play draws on Greek theater with its limited number of actors, its crises always offstage, and its absent divinity;

on Noh theater with its symbolic tree, its nuances and its ritual dance; on *commedia dell'arte,* improvised before our eyes; on twentieth-century experimental theater; and on vaudeville with its castoff clowns, stumblings, shamblings, delicate bawdry, acrobatics, and astringent pointlessness. The final action partakes of the circus repertoire

> (*They each take an end of the cord and pull. It breaks. They almost fall*),

synchronized with a burlesque house misadventure with trousers

> . . . *which, much too big for him, fall about his ankles.*

The student of *Finnegans Wake* will identify this mishap as the play's epiphany[2], the least learned will note that something hitherto invisible has at last been disclosed, and everyone can agree that the final gesture is to a static propriety:

VLADIMIR: Pull ON your trousers.
ESTRAGON: (*realizing his trousers are down*). True.
    He pulls up his trousers.
VLADIMIR: Well? Shall we go?
ESTRAGON: Yes, let's go.
    They do not move.

Curtain.

2

This superimposition of dramatic economies was not achieved at once. About 1947, just after writing the *Nouvelles,* Beckett occupied himself with a radically

---

[2] Cf. *Finnegans Wake,* p. 508: ". . . I am sorry to have to tell you, hullo and evoe, they were coming down from off him. —How culious an epiphany!"

misconceived dramatic enterprise, a play called *Eleu-theria* in three acts, which entailed a large stage, two sets simultaneously on view, a place (Paris) and a time (three consecutive winter afternoons) uncharacteristically spec-ified, and seventeen speaking parts, including a Chinese torturer, an officious member of the audience, and the prompter. "Eleutheria" means "freedom." The theme, clearly related to that of the first *Nouvelle*, "L'Expulsé," concerns a young man's act of secession from his in-tensely bourgeois family. This theme preoccupied Beckett a good deal at one time; it also underlies the remarkable fragment, "From an Abandoned Work":

> Up bright and early that day, I was young then, feeling awful, and out, mother hanging out of the window in her nightdress weeping and waving. Nice fresh morn-ing, bright too early as so often. Feeling really awful, very violent. . . .

In the play, the family (surnamed Krap) entertains guests (named Piouk and Meck) and the conversation goes like this:

MR KRAP: Have a cigar.
DR PIOUK: Thank you.
MR KRAP: Yes thank you or no thank you?
DR PIOUK: I don't smoke.

(Silence)

MRS MECK }
MRS PIOUK } (*Together*): I . . .
MRS MECK: Oh, I beg your pardon. You were going to say?
MRS PIOUK: Oh, nothing. Go on.

(Silence)

Or ailments are discussed:

MRS PIOUK: How is Henry?
MRS KRAP: Ill.
MRS PIOUK: What's wrong with him?
MRS KRAP: I don't know. He's stopped urinating.
MRS PIOUK: It's the prostate.

Such details, however, lack the fine formal emptiness of *Godot*, partly because they occur in the interstices of an elaborate exposition of familial relationships. Beckett drags the audience, with considerable distaste, up and down all the airshafts of a well-made play. It is from this that Krap *fils*, the young Victor, has absented himself. He scrounges in trash cans, speaks to no one, and is generally found in bed, in a garret flat.

All the rest of the play—two mortal acts—is devoted to punching and poking Victor, in his garret, and beseeching him to explain his conduct. This he will not do, one aspect of his freedom, we may suppose, being freedom from the necessity to devise explanations, even for his own enlightenment. The busybodies include not only Victor's parents, their relatives, and his fiancée (a certain Mlle. Skunk), but also an officious artisan who is on the premises to repair a broken window, and who constitutes himself spokesman of detached practicality. By the third act an exasperated member of the audience has taken up his seat on the stage, determined to see things resolved before midnight; the services of an Oriental torturer have been requisitioned; Victor has made a statement, later retracted as fiction; and alone at last on the bare stage he has lain down "with his back turned to humanity."

Since the figure of interest (and on the stage, not of much interest) has by definition withdrawn from communication, Beckett's problem is, as never before, to fill up the work. To this end he employs, with little conviction, the convention of formal dramatic structure, which is that when someone speaks someone else answers, more or less to the point. And this convention closes round Victor like water round a stone, incapable of assimilating him.

Though it doesn't work in this play, the strategy is not new. All Beckett's writings bring some sustained formal element to the service of some irreducible situation round which the lucid sentences defile in baffled aplomb. If we never understand the world of Watt, that is not because the presentation conceals it; as the presence of irrational terms does not prevent us from following every line of a computation. So in *Molloy* the twin circular journeys, and in *Malone Dies* the parallel narratives, supply the words with something formal to disclose, and circumscribe the implacable mysteries. *Godot* for the same reason is full of small rituals and transparent local rhythms. They are not the mystery, they do not clarify the mystery, or seek to clarify the mystery, they clarify the place where the mystery is, and the fact that, in the presence of the irreducible, people contrive to kill time by rehearsing their grasp of detail.

Let us be clear about this. Victor is not a new moral phenomenon. Beckett has been concerned with the withdrawn man from Belacqua onward. Nor is he structurally a new component. He is this play's version of the familiar surd, the irreducible element which no style, no clarity, no ceremony will dissolve or explain: the thing which makes itself felt, in Beckett's cosmos, as a prevailing and penetrating mystery, seeping through the walls of stage or book. This mystery, this irreducible, is generally of two sorts: (1) in the domain of existence, the implacable *"d'être là"*: as we find ourselves situated on earth ("There's no cure for that") or as Malone finds himself placed in his mysterious room, surrounded by procedures that appear to take no account of his arrival or presence. Or (2) in the domain of will, the arbitrary decision, Molloy's determination to visit his mother, or Victor's to leave home. There is no looking into these

sudden precipitations. In large, they make contact with
the ambient terror and oppressiveness (what compels us
to wait for Godot?). In small, they supply a repertory of
comic effects. Part of the trouble with Victor in *Eleutheria*
is that his presence confuses these perspectives; his sulki-
ness verges on being funny at the same time that his in-
transigence is growing unnerving; he can round on his
inquistors by asking them why it is that they find him of
such consuming interest, when cripples, fools, nuns, and
other outcasts barely detain them.

In the *Nouvelles*, three of which Beckett published
though he had the sense not to publish *Eleutheria*, such
problems of tact do not arise. "L'Expulsé," a sort of Victor,
has generally preferred to keep to his room, and by
preference the end of the room where the bed is, so much
so that he barely knows the streets of his native town. At
the beginning of the story he is recalling how his family
finally threw him out.

> Even as I fell I heard the door slam, which brought me
> a little comfort, in the midst of my fall. For that meant
> they were not pursuing me down into the street, with a
> stick, to beat me in full view of the passers-by. For if that
> had been their intention they would not have closed the
> door, but left it open, so that the persons assembled in
> the vestibule might enjoy my chastisement and be edi-
> fied. So, for once, they had confined themselves to
> throwing me out, and no more about it. I had time, be-
> fore coming to rest in the gutter, to conclude this piece
> of reasoning.
> Under these circumstances nothing compelled me to get
> up immediately. I rested my elbow on the sidewalk, funny
> the things you remember, settled my ear in the cup of my
> hand and began to reflect on my situation, notwithstanding
> its familiarity. But the sound, fainter but unmistakable,
> of the door slammed again, roused me from my reverie,
> where already a whole landscape was taking form,
> charming with hawthorn and wild roses, most dreamlike,

and made me look up in alarm, my hands flat on the sidewalk and my legs braced for flight. But it was merely my hat, sailing towards me through the air, rotating as it came. I caught it and put it on. They were most correct, according to their god. They could have kept this hat, but it was not theirs, it was mine, so they gave it back to me. But the spell was broken.

And the life from which he has been expelled is adequately summed up by the hat:

> How describe this hat? And why? When my head had attained I shall not say its definitive but its maximum dimensions, my father said to me, Come, son, we are going to buy your hat, as though it had pre-existed from time immemorial in a pre-established place. He went straight to the hat. I personally had no say in the matter, nor had the hatter. I have often wondered if my father's purpose was not to humiliate me, if he was not jealous of me who was young and handsome, fresh at least, while he was already old and all bloated and purple. It was forbidden me, from that day forth, to go out bareheaded, my pretty brown hair blowing in the wind. Sometimes, in a secluded street, I took it off and held it in my hand, but trembling. I was required to brush it morning and evening. Boys my age with whom, in spite of everything. I was obliged to mix occasionally, mocked me. But I said to myself, it is not really the hat, they simply make merry at the hat because it is a little more glaring than the rest, for they have no finesse. I have always been amazed by my contemporaries' lack of finesse, I whose soul writhed from morning to night, in the mere quest of itself. But perhaps they were simply being kind, like those who make game of the hunchback's big nose. When my father died I could have got rid of this hat, there was nothing more to prevent me, but not I. But how describe it? Some other time, some other time.

This precious youth turns slowly into a bum. In "Premier Amour" (which was never published) he is living in an abandoned stable and devoted to "cerebral supinity, the deadening of the idea of the me and the idea of that small residue of exasperating trifles known as the not-me." Near the canal he comes to be frequented by a certain Lulu.

> Yes, I loved her, that was the name which I gave, and which alas I still give, to what I did, at that period. I possessed no data on the subject, not having previously loved, but I had heard the thing spoken of, naturally, at home, at school, in the brothel, and at church, and I had read romances, in prose and in verse, under the direction of my tutor, in English, French, Italian and German, in which it was spoken highly of. I was therefore well prepared to give a name to what I did, when I discovered myself writing the word Lulu on an old cowpad, or lying in the mud beneath the moon trying to pull up dandelions without breaking the stems.

His idyll, like Molloy's, is of short duration. All he really wants of her is a peaceable shelter, and he finds her clients disturbing. At the beginning of "Le Calmant" he (if it is still he) announces that he no longer knows when he died (whatever that means). He is quite likely in a hospital ("among these assassins, in a bed of terror"), but prefers to imagine himself in his distant refuge, hands clasped, head down, feeble, panting, calm, free, and "older than I could ever have been, if my calculations are correct." He tells himself a story of a nighttime ramble, maybe a real one, in which people came up against him like apparitions and talked no sense that he could follow, and a vision finally came to him of asphalt bursting into infinite flower, while he lay on the pavement immersed in his dream, and people took care not to step on him ("a considerateness which touched me"). In "The End" he is thrown out of the institution which has been harboring him, and after bizarre wanderings takes refuge at last in an abandoned canoe, where he dreams of slowly foundering in the open main, as the water rises slowly through a hole from which with his penknife he has extracted the cork.

All this is capital material for fiction, but not for drama. Since its point is that the protagonist has sundered all relation, so far as he can, with other persons and things, there is simply no way to exhibit him on the stage. The only thing to exhibit is other folks' curiosity about him, which grows tedious. And since Beckett's unwavering concern is with the twilight man, who does not inhabit the rational domain, whom you cannot see with Pythagorean eyes and for whom our moral vocabulary contains only the summary provided in the last sentence of "The End," that he has neither "the courage to stop nor the strength to go on," it would seem clear that for Beckett the drama was a hopeless form. But we know our man by this time; nothing makes him prick up his ears like the word "hopeless." Jettisoning *Eleutheria*, he gave over trying to dramatize the *Nouvelles* and commenced turning them instead into the trilogy. There is no telling whether it was pondering Molloy and Moran that suggested raising the number of idlers to two, for dialogue, and reducing the number of busy folk to two, for concision, and playing a waiting against a journeying, for structure. At any rate, after finishing *Molloy*, perhaps also *Malone Dies*[3], he commenced the impossible play, its two twilight men and much of the quality of their talk transposed from another jettisoned fiction, *Mercier et Camier*.

3

The two men waiting for Godot to come (or for night to fall) are very similar to the two men who were seeking

[3] Eleven years later he couldn't be sure. "Round about 1948 in any case."

to retrieve a bicycle and a haversack, on the off chance that these articles might prove relevant to their needs. Hear them one rainy morning discoursing of their umbrella:

> For myself, said Camier, I would not open it.
> And might we hear the reason? said Mercier. It is raining steadily, it seems to me. You are all wet.
> Your advice would be to open it? said Camier.
> I do not say that, said Mercier. I only ask when we are going to open it if we do not open it now.

This futile parasol deserves a moment's attention; there is nothing like it in *Godot*. Formerly red, tipped by a betasseled amber ball, it had floated down time's stream for nearly a half century before getting lodged in the junkshop where Mercier gave ninepence for it.

> It must have made its debut about 1900, said Camier. That was I think the year of Ladysmith, on the Klip. Do you remember it? A splendid time. Garden parties every day. Life opened before us, radiant. All hopes were permissible. We played at sieges. People die like flies. Hunger. Thirst. Bang! Bang! The last cartridges. Surrender! Never! We eat corpses. We drink our own urine. Bang! Bang! We kept two in reserve. What do we hear? A cry of wonder. Dust on the horizon. The column! Tongues are black. Hurrah anyhow! Rah! Rah! We sounded like ravens. A garrison marshal died of joy. We are saved. The century was two months old.
> Look at it now, said Mercier.

Look at the parasol now, or look at the century. Or look at us:

> How are you feeling? said Camier. I keep forgetting to ask.
> I felt well coming downstairs, said Mercier. Now I feel less well. Screwed up, if you like, but not to the sticking-place. And you?
> A chip, said Camier, in the midst of the limitless ocean.

Souvenir from the great dawn of an ampler day, when garden parties and rescue parties bespoke man's limitless hope, our parasol (bits of fringe still ornamenting its perimeter) is irrelevant to a time of rain, middle age, and doubt. For two pages they debate throwing it away, a course for which, Mercier concludes, it will perhaps be time "when it can no longer serve us for shelter, because of wear, or when we have achieved the certainty that between it and our present distress there has never existed the least relationship."

Very well, said Camier. But it is not sufficient to know that we shall not throw it away. It is equally needful to know whether we are to open it.

Since it is in part with a view to opening it that we are not throwing it away, said Mercier.

I know, I know, said Camier, but are we to open it immediately or wait until the weather has characterized itself more fully?

Mercier scrutinized the impenetrable sky.

Go and take a look, he said. Tell me what you think.

Camier went out into the street. He pressed on to the corner, so that Mercier lost sight of him. On returning, he said,

There may be clearing patches lower down. Would you like me to go up on the roof?

Mercier concentrated. Finally he said, impulsively,

Open it, for the love of God.

But Camier could not open it. The bitch, he said, it is stuck again.

Give it here, said Mercier.

But Mercier was no more fortunate. He brandished it. But he got himself in hand just in time. Proverb.

What have we done to God? he said.

We have denied him, said Camier.

You will not make me believe that his rancor goes to these lengths, said Mercier.

Tatter their clothing, divest the surrounding space of streets and houses, empty their hands of objects boasting assignable provenance, and they turn easily into Vladimir and Estragon. Between this dialogue and Didi's account of opportunities missed "il y a une éternité, vers 1900" (the less elegiac English text has "a million years ago, in the nineties") —

> Hand in hand from the top of the Eiffel Tower, among the first. We were respectable in those days. Now it's too late. They wouldn't even let us up.

—between Camier's mock Ladysmith and this, what differences of feeling we may discover radiate from the fact that Mercier and Camier have actually in their hands a relic of those times, whereas Didi must make do with memory, and Gogo (who can barely remember the previous day) with Didi's account. Their only possessions are their clothes. Certain of these are involved in the action: two hats (exchanged), one pair of boots (substituted for another), one pair of trousers (falling down), one rope, serving Estragon as a belt (broken). None of them has any history, none bespeaks any past. Indeed all are interchangeable with substitutes in some economy exterior to the action on the stage, as it seems clear that Estragon's trousers served someone of ampler build before they came to him. So much for objects. We may note the presence of food (turnips, carrots, radishes). The universe is also furnished with natural splendors (one tree) and natural phenomena (twilight, darkness, moonlight). Consequently its inhabitants are thrown completely on their own resources:

> VLADIMIR: You must be happy, too, deep down, if you only knew it.
> ESTRAGON: Happy about what?
> VLADIMIR: To be back with me again.
> ESTRAGON: Would you say so?
> VLADIMIR: Say you are, even if it's not true.
> ESTRAGON: What am I to say?
> VLADIMIR: Say, I am happy.

ESTRAGON: I am happy.
VLADIMIR: So am I.
ESTRAGON: So am I.
VLADIMIR: We are happy.
ESTRAGON: We are happy. (*Silence.*) What do we do,
now that we are happy?
VLADIMIR: Wait for Godot. (*Estragon groans. Silence.*)

There is one other difference between this world and
that of Mercier and Camier. The difference is named Godot:
another person, who matters. Whether or not he appears,
he supplies tensions no umbrella, bicycle, or haversack can
exert. In the play before us these tensions are barely
sketched; Beckett was not to concern himself with them
until more than a decade later, in *Embers* and *Comment
C'est*.

It is more our present business to note why, in transforming the ambiguously aimless journey of the novel
into the ambiguously empty waiting of the play, Beckett
has emptied the protagonists' world of objects. Objects,
in his universe, go with a journey: bicycles, for instance,
crutches, a hat secured by a string; in *Comment C'est*, a
jute sack, tins of fish, a can opener, used in the journeying, absent in the waiting. The objects Malone inventories
in his immobility—a needle stuck into two corks, the bowl
of a pipe, equipped with a little tin lid, a scrap of newspaper, a photograph of an ass wearing a boater—these
constitute no exception, for Malone's immobility is not
a waiting but by definition a terminal phase in a journey,
toward nothingness. Thus Malone's objects have histories.
Since they joined his entourage they have made a journey
through time in his company, undergoing modifications
not always at random (he knows under what circumstances the brim came off his hat; he removed it himself,
so that he might keep the hat on while he slept). It is
even possible to speculate concerning their pre-Malone

history; the pipe bowl which he found in the grass must have been thrown away by a man who said, when the stem broke, "Bah, I'll buy myself another." ("But all that is mere supposition.") Thus the static object, like Malone's own immobility, is a momentary cross section of a duration, the present index of a movement in time which may parallel or continue movement in space, as the Beckett journey is apt to become identical with the process of being alive.

But the scanty tale of objects that concern the bums in *Waiting for Godot* contains no item owning a past, a future, or a duration with which our vital sentiments may feel empathy. Like the elements at the beginning of a mathematical problem, the bowler hats, the boots, the pants, the rope, the tree are simply *given*, and the operations that are performed on them do not modify them (as, at the end of the most prolonged computation, x is still x).

There are, it is true, in the play a few things that undergo changes of a different order. These are irreversible changes, the sort prescribed by the Second Law of Thermodynamics, the law with whose gross effects Lucky's great speech is concerned. Reversible events are trivial, like rearrangements of furniture, or of the terms in an equation. By this criterion the status of most of the events in the play is slight, or at most ambiguous. Irreversible things are the ones that *happen*, that declare something more than a system of tautologies, or an economy of displacements. It is the sum of those happenings, however small, whose terms and agents can never again be put back the way they were—the carrot uneaten, the leaves unbudded—that advances by today's quantum the system's articulation, or perhaps its entropy. Of these *Waiting for Godot* contains a real but insignificant number.

Though this is the play in which, as Vivian Mercier

wittily observed, "nothing happens, twice," things at the fall of the final curtain are not precisely as they were. Before our eyes a carrot has come into visibility out of Didi's pocket and vanished again into Gogo's mouth; its subsequent decomposition may be conjectured. Before our eyes, also, the rope has been broken, into two pieces whose combined length will equal the original length, but which can never again be combined. These are both irreversible actions; the world is now poorer by one carrot and one rope. In the interval between the acts there have been three organic changes: the tree has acquired leaves, and Pozzo has lost his sight and Lucky his speech. (We have only Pozzo's word for the latter two). It is not clear whether these count as irreversible events, though certainly the leaves cannot be expected to go back into the tree. In the same interval Gogo's boots have been taken, and a pair of a different color substituted. Didi ventures an explanation of this, inaccurate because based on inadequate data. With the benefit of our later knowledge that the new boots are larger than the old, we can readily amend his hypothesis. The play's other substitution occurs before our eyes: as a result of a sequence of permutations too long to reconstruct, Didi midway through Act II has Lucky's hat on his head, and Didi's hat has replaced Lucky's on the ground. And one further item comes from outside the visible economy of the play, viz. Lucky's second hat, the hat he is wearing on his reappearance in Act II, after having left his first hat on the ground before his exit in Act. I. These substitutions are presumably reversible, though it is not clear how Lucky's second hat would have to be disposed of.

Nor can the tedium of two evenings be said to redeem its own nullity by enhancing the experience of Didi and Gogo, as one may learn by watching bees move about.

They exist in an eternity of stagnation, Gogo's memory defective ("Either I forget immediately or I never forget"), Didi's an eventless assimilation of the same to the remembered same. They are, unlike Murphy, Mercier, Molloy, Moran, and Malone, utterly incapable of the kind of experience you can later tell a story about, and utterly detached from the least affection for objects. They have only their bodies and their clothes: hence the mathematical speed with which their situation can be exhibited. Not having chosen suicide ("sans le courage de finir ni la force de continuer"), they have grown committed, in a kind of fierce negative sanctity, to waiting for the figure with sheep, goats, many affairs, and a white beard (we need not credit any of these details). Their lives correspond exactly to St. John of the Cross's famous minimal prescription, divested of the love of created things, and the divine union is awaited beside the tree, one evening, another evening—every evening, since two terms, in the absence of indications to the contrary, imply a series, perhaps infinite. They are blessed, says Didi, in knowng the answer to the question, what it is they are doing there. They are waiting for Godot to come, or for night to fall. They have kept their appointment, that too they can claim, and it is not by accident that he refers to the saints. "We are not saints, but we have kept our appointment. How many people can boast as much?"

Lest we be tempted to take this rhetorical question for the ridge pole of the play, Gogo replies, "Billions," and Didi concedes that he may be right. The question, climaxing the longest speech either of them is to deliver, retains its torque.

Having reduced the whole of two men's lives to a waiting which epitomizes a moral issue, Beckett causes this situation to be intersected by his other key situation, a journey. Pozzo and Lucky are a little like Moran and his son, seen from the outside instead of through Moran's narrative. They are loaded, as if to emphasize the distinction between waiters and travelers, with every kind of portable property, notably a heavy bag (of sand), a folding stool, a picnic basket (with chicken and wine), a greatcoat, a whip, a watch (genuine half-hunter, with deadbeat escapement,[4] gift of Pozzo's grandfather), a handkerchief, a pocket vaporizer, a rope, glasses, matches, and a briar pipe (by Kapp and Peterson). The watch is often consulted; there is a schedule to observe. If these two, master and servant, steadily on the move, epitomize the busy world from which Didi and Gogo have seceded, there is no record of the act of secession. Rather, the contrasting pairs appear to epitomize not ways of life so much as modes of being. Amid the great void which they contrive to fill up with exercises and conversation, Didi and Gogo circulate about one another with numb but delectable affection, Didi perpetually responsible for Gogo, enraged when Gogo is kicked, and offering to carry him (*Pause*) "if necessary." Gogo for his part rejects a proposed system for hanging themselves on the sole ground, he says, that if it fails his friend will be left alone. Both strike noble if temporary rages on behalf of Lucky, and even, when Lucky is put in the wrong, on behalf of Pozzo; and with infinite delay and ratiocination they do eventually help the blind Pozzo of the second act to his feet. Pozzo, on the other hand, absurd, theatrical, glib, patronizing ("so that I ask myself is there anything I can do in my turn for these honest fellows who are having such a dull, dull time") is capable of nothing but stage turns: the judicious stranger, the picnicker at his

---

[4] See Abbot Payson Usher, *A History of Mechanical Inventions*, chap. xii, p. 313

ease, the eulogist of twilight, the man whose heart goes pit-a-pat—very much, in each of his roles, someone we have seen before. This kaleidoscope of impostors learned all that he knows from Lucky, and we are given at some length a specimen of Lucky's capacity for imparting the things he has in his head. They live with their heads, these two, moving hither and thither, Pozzo talking of buying and selling, and imposing with his campstool and ceremonial a prissy elegance on their halts; Lucky treacherous, miserable, obeying with a precision that does not quite approximate to ritual, and dancing or thinking on command. There is no love here, and the play's waiting seems incontestably preferable to its journeying.

4

For the stage is a place to wait. The place itself waits, when no one is in it. When the curtain rises on *Endgame*, sheets drape all visible objects as in a furniture warehouse. Clov's first act is to uncurtain the two high windows and inspect the universe; his second is to remove the sheets and fold them carefully over his arm, disclosing two ash cans and a figure in an armchair. This is so plainly a metaphor for waking up that we fancy the stage, with its high peepholes, to be the inside of an immense skull. It is also a ritual for starting the play; Yeats arranged such a ritual for *At the Hawk's Well*, and specified a black cloth and a symbolic song. It is finally a removal from symbolic storage of the objects that will be needed during the course of the performance. When the theater is empty it is sensible to keep them covered against dust. So we are reminded at the outset that what we are to witness is a dusty dramatic exhibition, repeated and repeatable. The necessary objects include

three additional players (two of them in ash cans). Since
none of them will move from his station we can think of
them after the performance as being kept permanently on
stage, and covered with their dust cloths again until tomorrow night.

The rising of the curtain disclosed these sheeted forms;
the removal of the sheets disclosed the protagonist and
his ash cans; the next stage is for the protagonist to un-
cover his own face, which he does with a yawn, culmi-
nating this three-phase strip tease with the revelation of a
very red face and black glasses. His name, we gather from
the program, is Hamm, a name for an actor. He is also
Hamlet, bounded in a nutshell, fancying himself king of
infinite space, but troubled by bad dreams; he is also "a
toppled Prospero,"[5] remarking partway through the play,
with judicious pedantry, "our revels now are ended";
he is also the Hammer to which Clov, Nagg and Nell (Fr.
clou, Ger. *Nagel,* Eng. *nail*) stand in passive relationship;
by extension, a chess player ("Me—[*he yawns*]—to play");
but also (since Clov must wheel him about) himself a
chessman, probably the imperiled King.

Nagg and Nell in their dustbins appear to be pawns;
Clov, with his arbitrarily restricted movements ("I can't
sit.") and his equestrian background ("And your rounds?
Always on foot?" "Sometimes on horse.") resembles the
Knight, and his perfectly cubical kitchen ("ten feet by
ten feet by ten feet, nice dimensions,· nice proportions")
resembles a square on the chessboard translated into
three dimensions. He moves back and forth, into it and
out of it, coming to the succor of Hamm and then retreating. At the endgame's end the pawns are forever immobile and Clov is poised for a last departure from the

5 This admirable phrase is Mr. Roy Walker's, in the December 1958
Twentieth Century.

board, the status quo forever menaced by an expected piece glimpsed through the window, and King Hamm abandoned in check:

> Old endgame lost of old, play and lose and have done with losing. . . . Since that's the way we're playing it, let's play it that way . . . and speak no more about it . . . speak no more.

Even if we had not the information that the author of this work has been known to spend hours playing chess with himself (a game at which you always lose[6]), we should have been alerted to his long-standing interest in its strategy by the eleventh chapter of *Murphy*, where Murphy's first move against Mr. Endon, the standard P—K$_4$, is described as "the primary cause of all [his] subsequent difficulties." (The same might be said of getting born, an equally conventional opening.) Chess has several peculiarities which lend themselves to the metaphors of this jagged play. It is a game of leverage, in which the significance of a move may be out of all proportion to the local disturbance it effects ("A flea! This is awful! What a day!"). It is a game of silences, in which new situations are appraised: hence Beckett's most frequent stage direction, "*Pause.*" It is a game of steady attrition; by the time we reach the endgame the board is nearly bare, as bare as Hamm's world where there are no more bicycle wheels, sugarplums, pain killers, or coffins, let alone people. And it is a game which by the successive removal of screening pieces constantly extends the range of lethal forces, until at the endgame peril from a key piece sweeps down whole ranks and files. The king is hobbled by the rule which allows him to move in any direction but only one square at a time; Hamm's circuit of the stage and re-

---

6 Or always win. "One of the thieves was saved. It's a reasonable percentage."

turn to center perhaps exhibits him patrolling the inner boundaries of the little nine-square territory he commands. To venture further will evidently expose him to check. ("Outside of here it's death.") His knight shuttles to and fro, his pawns are pinned. No threat is anticipated from the auditorium, which is presumably off the board; and a periodic reconnaissance downfield through the windows discloses nothing but desolation until very near the end. But on his last inspection of the field Clov is dismayed. Here the English text is inexplicably sketchy; in the French one we have,

> CLOV: Aïeaïeaïe!
> HAMM: C'est une feuille? Une fleur? Une toma— (il bâille) —te?
> CLOV: (regardant) Je t'en foutrai des tomates! Quelqu'un! C'est quelqu'un!
> HAMM: Eh bien, va l'exterminer. (Clov descend de l'escabeau.) Quelqu'un! (Vibrant.) Fais ton devoir!

In the subsequent interrogatory we learn the distance of this threat (fifteen meters or so), its state of rest or motion (motionless), its sex (presumably a boy), its occupation (sitting on the ground as if leaning on something). Hamm, perhaps thinking of the resurrected Jesus, murmurs "La pierre levée," then on reflection changes the image to constitute himself proprietor of the Promised Land: "Il regarde la maison sans doute, avec les yeux de Moïse mourant." It is doing, however, nothing of the kind; it is gazing at its navel. There is no use, Hamm decides, in running out to exterminate it: "If he exists he'll die there or he'll come here. And if he doesn't . . ." And a few seconds later he has conceded the game:

> It's the end, Clov, we've come to the end. I don't need you any more.

He sacrifices his last mobile piece, discards his staff and whistle, summons for the last time a resourceless Knight and an unanswering Pawn, and covers his face once more with the handkerchief: somehow in check.

Not that all this is likely to be yielded up with clarity by any conceivable performance. It represents however a structure which, however we glimpse it, serves to refrigerate the incidental passions of a play about, it would seem, the end of humanity. It is not for nothing that the place within which the frigid events are transacted is more than once called "the shelter," outside of which is death; nor that the human race is at present reduced to two disabled parents, a macabre blind son, and an acathisiac servant. Around this shelter the universe crumbles away like an immense dry biscuit: no more rugs, no more tide, no more coffins. We hear of particular deaths:

> CLOV (*harshly*): When old Mother Pegg asked you for oil or her lamp and you told her to get out to hell, you knew what was happening then, no? (*Pause.*) You know what she died of, Mother Pegg? Of darkness.
> HAMM (*feebly*): I hadn't any.
> CLOV (*as before*): Yes, you had.

We observe particular brutalities: Hamm, of his parents: "Have you bottled her?" "Yes." "Are they both bottled?" "Yes." "Screw down the lids." What has shrunken the formerly ample world is perhaps Hamm's withdrawal of love; the great skull-like setting suggests a solipsist's universe. "I was never there," he says. "Absent, always. It all happened without me. I don't know what's happened." He has been in "the shelter"; he has also been closed within himself. It is barely possible that the desolation is not universal:

> HAMM: Did you ever think of one thing?
> CLOV: Never.
> HAMM: That here we're down in a hole. (*Pause.*) But

> beyond the hills? Eh? Perhaps it's still green. Eh?
> (*Pause.*) Flora! Pomona! (*Ecstatically.*) Ceres!
> (*Pause.*) Perhaps you won't need to go very far.
> CLOV: I can't go very far. (*Pause.*) I'll leave you.

As Hamm is both chessman and chess player, so it is conceivable that destruction is not screened off by the shelter but radiates from it for a certain distance. Zero, zero, words we hear so often in the dialogue, these are the Cartesian coordinates of the origin.

Bounded in a nutshell yet king of infinite space, Hamm articulates the racking ambiguity of the play by means of his dominance over its most persuasive metaphor, the play itself. If he is Prospero with staff and revels, if he is Richard III bloodsmeared and crying "My kingdom for a nightman!" if he is also perhaps Richard II, within whose hollow crown

> . . . Keeps Death his court, and there the Antic sits,
> Scoffing his state and grinning at his pomp,
> Allowing him a breath, a little scene
> To monarchize, be feared, and kill with looks—[7]

these roles do not exhaust his repertoire. He is (his name tells us) the generic Actor, a creature all circumference and no center. As master of the revels, he himself attends to the last unveiling of the opening ritual:

> (*Pause. Hamm stirs. He yawns under the handkerchief. He removes the handkerchief from his face. Very red face, black glasses.*)
> HAMM: Me— (*he yawns*) —to play. (*He holds the handkerchief spread out before him.*) Old stancher! (. . . *He clears his throat, joins the tips of his fingers.*) Can there be misery— (*he yawns*)—loftier than mine?

The play ended, he ceremoniously unfolds the handkerchief once more (five separate stage directions govern-

---

7 I owe this suggestion to Mr. Walker's article.

ing his tempo) and covers his face as it was in the beginning. "Old Stancher! (*Pause.*) You . . . remain." What remains, in the final brief tableau specified by the author, is the immobile figure with a bloodied Veronica's veil in place of a face: the actor having superintended his own Passion and translated himself into an ultimate abstraction of masked agony.

Between these termini he animates everything, ordering the coming and going of Clov and the capping and uncapping of the cans. When Clov asks, "What is there to keep me here?" he answers sharply, "The dialogue." A particularly futile bit of business with the spyglass and the steps elicits from him an aesthetic judgment, "This is deadly." When it is time for the introduction of the stuffed dog, he notes, "We're getting on," and a few minutes later, "Do you not think this has gone on long enough?" These, like comparable details in *Godot*, are sardonic authorizations for a disquiet that is certainly stirring in the auditorium. No one understands better than Beckett, nor exploits more boldly, the kind of fatalistic attention an audience trained on films is accustomed to place at the dramatist's disposal. The cinema has taught us to suppose that a dramatic presentation moves inexorably as the reels unwind or the studio clock creeps, until it has consumed precisely its allotted time which nothing, no restlessness in the pit, no sirens, no mass exodus can hurry. "Something is taking its course," that suffices us. Hence the vast leisure in which the minimal business of *Godot* and *Endgame* is transacted; hence (transposing into dramatic terms the author's characteristic pedantry of means) the occasional lingering over points of technique, secure in the knowledge that the clock-bound patience of a twentieth-century audience will expect no inner urgency, nothing in fact but the actual time events consume, to determine the pace of the exhibition. Clov asks, "Why this farce, day after day?" and it is sufficient for Hamm to reply, "Routine. One never knows." It is the answer of an actor in an age of films and long runs. In *Endgame* (which here differs radically from *Godot*) no one is supposed to be improvising; the script has been well committed to memory and well rehearsed. By this means doom is caused to penetrate the most intimate crevices of the play. "I'm tired of going on," says Clov late in the play, "very tired," and then, "Let's stop playing!" (if there is one thing that modern acting is not it is playing). In the final moments theatrical technique, under Hamm's sponsorship, rises into savage prominence.

> HAMM: . . . And me? Did anyone ever have pity on me?
> CLOV: (*lowering the telescope, turning towards Hamm*): What? (*Pause.*) Is it me you're referring to?
> HAMM: (*angrily*): An aside, ape! Did you never hear an aside before? (*Pause.*) I'm warming up for my last soliloquy.

Ten seconds later he glosses "More complications!" as a technical term: "Not an underplot, I trust." It is Clov who has the last word in this vein:

> HAMM: Clov! (*Clov halts, without turning.*) Nothing. (*Clov moves on.*) Clov! (*Clov halts, without turning.*)
> CLOV: This is what we call making an exit.

By this reiterated stress on the actors as professional men, and so on the play as an occasion within which they operate, Beckett transforms Hamm's last soliloquy into a performance, his desolation into something prepared by the dramatic machine, his abandoning of gaff, dog, and whistle into a necessary discarding of props, and the terminal business with the handkerchief into, quite literally, a curtain speech. *Endgame* ends with an unexpected lightness, a death rather mimed than experienced; if it is "Hamm as stated, and Clov as stated, together as stated," the mode of statement has more salience than a paraphrase of the play's situation would lead one to expect.

The professionalism also saves the play from an essentially sentimental committment to simpliste "destiny." Much of its gloomy power it derives from contact with such notions as T. H. Huxley's view of man as an irrelevance whom day by day an indifferent universe engages in chess. We do not belong here, runs a strain of Western thought which became especially articulate in France after the War; we belong nowhere; we are all surds, ab-surd. There is nothing on which to ground our right to exist, and we need not be especially surprised one day to find ourselves nearly extinct. (On such a despair Cartesian logic converges, as surely as the arithmetic of Pythagoras wedged itself fast in the irrationality of $\sqrt{2}$.) Whatever we do, then, since it can obtain no grip on our radically pointless situation, is *behavior* pure and simple; it is play acting, and may yield us the satisfaction, if satisfaction there be, of playing well, of uttering our *cris du coeur* with style and some sense of timing. We do not trouble deaf heaven, for there is only the sky ("Rien," reports Clov, gazing through his telescope; and again, "Zéro.") We stir and thrill, at best, ourselves. From such a climate, miscalled existentialist, Beckett wrings every available *frisson* without quite delivering the play into its keeping; for its credibility is not a principle the play postulates but an idea the play contains, an idea of which it works out the moral and spiritual consequences. The despair in which he traffics is a conviction, not a philosophy. He will even set it spinning like a catharine wheel about a wild point of logic, as when he has Hamm require that God be prayed to in silence

("Where are your manners?") and then berate him ("The bastard!") for not existing.[8]

The play contains whatever ideas we discern inside it; no idea contains the play. The play contains, moreover, two narrative intervals, performances within the performance. The first, Nagg's story about the trousers, is explicitly a recitation; Nell has heard it often, and so, probably, has the audience; it is a vaudeville standby. Nagg's performance, like a production of *King Lear*, whose story we know, must therefore be judged solely as a performance. Its quality, alas, discourages even him ("I tell this story worse and worse."), and Nell too is not amused, being occupied with thoughts of her own, about the sand at the bottom of Lake Como. The other is Hamm's huffe-snuffe narrative, also a recitation, since we are to gather that he has been composing it beforehand, in his head. This time we do not know the substance of the tale, but contemplate in diminishing perspective an actor who has memorized a script which enjoins him to imitate a man who has devised and memorized a script:

> The man came crawling towards me, on his belly. Pale, wonderfully pale and thin, he seemed on the point of— (*Pause. Normal tone.*) No, I've done that bit.

Later on he incorporates a few critical reflections: "Nicely put, that," or "There's English for you." This technician's narcissism somewhat disinfects the dreadful tale. All Hamm's satisfactions come from dramatic self-contemplation, and as he towers before us, devoid of mercy, it is to some ludicrous stage villain that he assimilates himself, there on the stage, striking a stage-Barabbas

---

8 The Lord Chamberlain, a less subtle (or less orthodox) theologian, required that for performances on the English stage "bastard" should be altered to "swine."

pose ("Sometimes I go about and poison wells.") It is to this
that life as play-acting comes.

> In the end he asked me would I consent to take in the
> child as well—if he were still alive. (*Pause.*) It was the
> moment I was waiting for. (*Pause.*) Would I consent to
> take in the child. . . . (*Pause.*) I can see him still, down
> on his knees, his hands flat on the ground, glaring at me
> with his mad eyes, in defiance of my wishes.

"It was the moment I was waiting for": the satisfaction
this exudes is considerably less sadistic than dramatic,
and the anticlimax into which the long performance
immediately topples would try a creator's soul, not a
maniac's:

> I'll soon have finished with this story. (*Pause.*) Unless
> I bring in other characters. (*Pause.*) But where would I
> find them? (*Pause.*) Where would I look for them?
> (*Pause. He whistles. Enter Clov.*) Let us pray to God.

So the hooks go in. There is no denying what Beckett
called in a letter to Alan Schneider "the power of the
text to claw." It strikes, however, its unique precarious
balance between rage and art, immobilizing all characters but one, rotating before us for ninety unbroken minutes the surfaces of Nothing, always designedly faltering
on the brink of utter insignificance into which nevertheless we cannot but project so many awful significances:
theater reduced to its elements in order that theatrical-
ism may explore without mediation its own boundaries:
a bleak unforgettable tour de force and probably its author's single most remarkable work.

Voices In The Dark

il arrive j'aurai une voix plus de voix au monde
que la mienne un murmure eu une vie là-haut ici
verrai de nouveau mes choses un peu de bleu sous
la boue un peu de blanc nos choses petites scènes
ciels surtout et chemins

— *Comment C'est*

If *Endgame* eviscerates stage drama (as the trilogy did
fiction) the better to inspect its entrails, the plays for radio that succeed *Endgame* abolish the stage and explore
the resources of a world created by voices. "All is a question of voices," reflects The Unnamable more than once.

> I'm in words, made of words, others' words, what others,
> the place too, the air, the walls, the floor, the ceiling, all
> words, the whole world is here with me, I'm the air, the
> walls, the walled-in one, everything yields, opens, ebbs,
> flows, like flakes, I'm all these flakes, meeting, mingling,
> falling asunder.

All this is strictly true of a character in fiction, but he
means more than that. He means too that man is man by
virtue of speech, and that all speech is an echoing of
echoes. This truth radio imitates more intimately than
the printed page. "I'm all these words, all these stran-
gers, this dust of words, with no ground for their settling":
such are the beings created by the loudspeaker, creating themselves instant by instant and vanishing when
they fall silent. "Do not imagine," says Mrs. Rooney after
four other voices have intervened in the twenty seconds
since her last speech, "do not imagine, because I am silent,
that I am not present, and alive, to all that is going on."

This is not simply Mrs. Rooney asserting her grievance, but radio drama asserting its nature, and Beckett turned to radio drama at a crest of preoccupation with the fact that for him to live was to make stories, creating with words beings not himself, but perfecting his own identity in perfecting their words.

In *All That Fall* the illusion of a populous, varied world is so remarkable that the dramatist must more than once remind us that it is illusion merely. He is at pains to remind us, because the play turns less on illusion than on its illusoriness, a purely aural landscape capitalizing eerily on the fact that whatever falls silent disappears. *All That Fall* is full of departures elsewhere, but "elsewhere," not being where our ears are, doesn't exist in the way that "offstage" exists. We can imagine Clov's kitchen ("ten feet by ten feet by ten feet") by a gesture of spatial extension to the right; but where is Mr. Slocum, after we hear the last grinding of his gears? What becomes of Mr. Tyler, Mr. Barrell, and Miss Fitt, after they have spoken for the last time, with half of the play still to be transacted? Where, for that matter, does Mr. Rooney come from, when his voice suddenly joins the consort? The death of the child, on which the structure of incident depends, occurred then in the *néant*; and the question whether Mr. Rooney was guilty is as meaningless as the question whether Pozzo is really Godot, or whether Hamm's savage want of love has really been the principle of dissolution in a universe now patently dissolving. For certainties, Beckett will not cease to tell us, are largely conventions and bounded by a mystery.

Mr. Rooney has come by train from the city, we are meant to understand; and as for the others, we have left them behind at the station; but there is no station, no train, no city, no movement in space; only the convention represented in the printed text by the direction, "Dragging feet, panting, thudding stick," and in the BBC production by an insistent metrical figure on the kettledrums.

The two radio plays, *All That Fall* and *Embers*, focus respectively on the two Beckett conditions, a moving and an immobility. *All That Fall* takes us the long journey to the station and back again, with a waiting between. People move, by cart, by bicycle, by limousine, by train, and on foot, dragging, limping, running. All these movements in space are translated by the aural medium into time, where sounds expend themselves and die. Things that always occur in time, meanwhile: transmogrifications, failings, vanishings; these are presented to us at every instant of the dialogue, so that the play is steeped in transience, a transience the more total because there is nothing whatever that we can see, no tree onstage for two hours, no windows, ash cans, or armchairs. All that fall, says the title; and all are falling. "How is your poor wife?" "No better, Ma'am." "Your daughter then?" "No worse, Ma'am." After a silence, "Nice day for the races, Ma'am." "No doubt it is. (*Pause.*) But will it hold up? (*Pause. With emotion.*) Will it hold up?" Five minutes later, with another interlocutor, "What news of your daughter?" "Fair, fair. They removed everything, you know, the whole . . . er . . . bag of tricks. Now I am grandchildless." A minute later: "It is suicide to be abroad. But what is it to be at home, Mr. Tyler, what is it to be at home? A lingering dissolution. Now we are white with dust from head to foot." As Malone does nothing but die, so in this play human beings have nothing to anticipate but decline. Mrs. Rooney has lost a daughter; were her daughter alive now, "In her forties now she'd be, I don't know, fifty, girding up her lovely little loins, getting ready for the change." Mrs. Rooney is "destroyed with sorrow and pining and gentility and church-going and fat and rheumatism." Mr. Rooney is now blind and anticipates with some relish going deaf and dumb. Mrs. Rooney's dress gets torn; a hen dies beneath Mr. Slocum's car. The car in turn declines to start until violent measures are taken. Most unnerving of all, the very bicycle (*maestro di color che vanno*) has ruptured a tire and bids fair to break its owner's heart: "Now if it were the front I should not so much mind. But the back. The back! The chain! The oil! The grease! The hub! The brakes! The gear! No! It is too much!" It is into a collective process of this kind that children are born.

Thus the mode in which the play itself exists, as a series of auditory effects in time, sustains its theme of transience. The very ditch, we are told, contains rotting leaves ("In June? Rotting leaves in June?" "Yes, dear, from last year, and from the year before last, and from the year before that again.") ; and the ditch itself is no more present to our senses than it is to blind Dan's: "What way am I facing?" "What?" "I have forgotten what way I am facing." "You have turned aside and are bowed down over the ditch." These words create the ditch, for us as for him; when they move on it has gone. We too are blind. Words, similarly, create the ephemerally substantial Mrs. Rooney herself, words and sounds, so vividly that the tour de force of the play consists in the elaborate illusion that her two hundred pounds of bulk are being shouldered by main force into a motor car. This hysterical scene ("Oh . . . Lower! . . . Don't be afraid! . . .We're past the age when . . . There! . . . Now! . . . Get your shoulder under it! . . . Oh! (*Giggles.*) Oh glory! . . . Up! Up! Ah! I'm in!") and its later counterpart the extraction scene ("Crouch down, Mrs. Rooney, crouch down and get your head in the open." "Crouch down! At my time of life! This is lunacy!") make her at the same time vastly substantial to the mind's eye, and vastly decrepit. Yet even Mrs. Rooney is an illusion; all living is an illusion; the very animals whose ways have not changed since Arcady are merely so many baas and bleats, manifestly generated by the sound effects department. (Beckett has said that he would have preferred the approximations of human imitators to the BBC's painstaking illusion.) Pulsating in acoustic space, the soundscape asserts a provisional reality, at every instant richly springing forth and dying.

The background of a play for voices is silence, a silence amidst which the specifically human asserts itself with a special torque. The words do not tumble forth, they are composed, and into sentences, whose Ionic elegance, even as the silence claims it, cries aloud to enter an immobility in which to be savored. "Let us halt a moment," says Mrs. Rooney, "and this vile dust fall back upon the viler worms." The very cries of her heart have a fine rhetorical finesse. ("Oh cursed corset! If I could let it out, without indecent exposure.") This extraordinary combination of vivacity and artifice, which accounts for much of the fascination of the play, does not fail in its turn to become conscious of itself. In the first few minutes we find Mrs. Rooney arrested by her own way of speaking (her word for it, itself a *trouvaille*, is "bizarre") ; and near the end Mr. Rooney restates this theme.

> MRS. ROONEY: No, no, I am agog, tell me all, then we shall press on and never pause, never pause, till we come safe to haven.
> (*Pause.*)
> MR. ROONEY: Never pause . . . safe to haven . . . Do you know, Maddy, sometimes one would think you were struggling with a dead language.

MRS. ROONEY: Yes indeed, Dan, I know full well what you mean, I often have that feeling, it is unspeakably excruciating.

MR. ROONEY: I confess I have it sometimes myself, when I happen to overhear what I am saying.

MRS. ROONEY: Well you know, it will be dead in time, just like our own poor dear Gaelic, there is that to be said.

This is a critical moment in the development of the play's theme. Language itself, it appears, is about to be assimilated into the utter transience the play has now been exploring for sixty minutes: all speech a struggle with dying idioms, and human dignity, which asserts itself in speech, an illusion readily swept away. Then a live language intervenes:

Urgent baa.

MR. ROONEY: (*startled.*) Good God!

MRS. ROONEY: Oh, the pretty little woolly lamb, crying to suck its mother! Theirs has not changed, since Arcady.

Arcady, a fictitious past; crying to suck its mother, a tissue of fictions; the pretty little woolly lamb, an anonymous invention, Mrs. Rooney's reality perhaps, but not a shepherd's nor for that matter a zoologist's (theirs too are fictions). Everything, at this moment, reels into unreliability except the sound of the baa (which has known no Grimm's law) and the fact that Mrs. Rooney has constructed another of her impassioned miniatures.

Pause.

MR. ROONEY: Where was I in my composition?

MRS. ROONEY: At a standstill.

MR. ROONEY: Ah yes. (*Clears his throat. Narrative tone.*) I concluded naturally that we had entered a station. . .

His long account of how things were on the train is a
"composition" also; "narrative tone" recalls Hamm's unending story, and Nagg's joke. For the work in hand to
scrutinize its own mode of being, and having suddenly
discerned the conventions upon which it is established
to suddenly cancel out all certainties by forcing on our
attention a converging series of fictions, as of mirrors
facing one another, this is a familiar Beckett technique.
It is finally the linchpin of the work that gathers up all
these lesser works of the late 1950's, *Comment C'est*. It
serves in *All That Fall* to remove into uncertainty forever
the question of Mr. Rooney's responsibility, conscious or
unconscious, for what happened to the little girl. It is useless to assemble clues. ("Did you ever wish to kill a child?"
. . . "I had the compartment to myself as usual. At least I
hope so, for I made no attempt to restrain myself." . . .
"Say something, Maddy. Say you believe me.") Useless,
because all facts are provisional except the fact that
sounds are being uttered. Everything is infected with fiction. Mr. Rooney, moreover, is as thoroughly as Murphy
divided between a mental life that expresses itself, if at
all, in objurgation and narrative, but prefers, presumably, revery ("I dream of other roads in other lands. Of
another home, another— (*he hesitates*) —another home.
(*Pause.*) What was I trying to say?"), and a bodily existence over which the mind has little control, and in which
it has little interest. What the dramatic medium compels
us to do is acquiesce in this indifference of expression to
fact; a sound or two, a word or two, we find, has the power
to make us believe virtually anything. So we can only
know what Mr. Rooney tells us, which may in turn be
the fiction he chooses to entertain himself with, like so
many Beckett characters. In the final moments we know
this much, that the train was late because a child fell

beneath the wheels (for even in radio plays one is to trust a messenger). It comes as a brutal and shocking fact, rupturing the elegiac tone and the inimitably gentle grotesquerie by which we have been suffused for seventy-five minutes. Until now the indomitable language has absorbed every human shock, and extracted from universal decay a species of melancholy satisfaction. But: "Under the wheels, ma'am." There is no reply. Not even Mrs. Rooney will be able to cope with this for several weeks. It is too terrible for apothegm, epigram, cadence, or plaint. The dead language with which she struggles and from which she wrests the satisfactions of eloquence is suddenly defeated by something intransigently alive: a death. So the play ends, as a dream may terminate in a gunshot, or as "Dante and the Lobster" closed with the dreadful words about a quick death: "It is not." It is open to doubt whether the effect quite coheres: for art has suddenly refused to be art and brought forward living pain.

Embers, on the other hand, Beckett's most difficult work, coheres to perfection, locking us as it does inside the word spinner's prison. There is only one voice for half its duration, Henry's, on the strand. ("That sound you hear is the sea, we are sitting on the strand. I mention it because the sound is so strange, so unlike the sound of the sea, that if you didn't see what it was you wouldn't know what it was.") Taking command of the medium in Hamm's way, he tells us this; so of course we can't be sure; for hooves sound when he calls for them, and the sea, it may be, is another such illusion. He is the director as well as the principal actor; the sound-effects men await his cues. He talks constantly; he talks, he tells us, to drown out the sea (which may not be there). Ada agrees that it may not be there ("You shouldn't be hearing it, there must be something wrong with your brain."), and Ada herself quite likely isn't there, since her voice enters the cosmos at his command, like those hooves. It is through several removes, therefore, that he arrives at the possibility that he may be deluded. He also comes sidewise at the bleakness of his own solipsism. This theme is broached by Ada's voice, which asks, "Who were you with just now? Before you spoke to me," to which he replies, "I was trying to be with my father." (His father he has earlier called "an old man blind and foolish. . . . My father, back from the dead, to be with me. . . . As if he hadn't died.") This is a sort of game he plays, just as Ada's voice, we come to understand, speaks out of a kind of game he plays. Her voice says:

> "I suppose you have worn him out. (*Pause.*) You wore him out living and now you are wearing him out dead. (*Pause.*) The time comes when one cannot speak to you any more. (*Pause.*) The time will come when no one will speak to you at all, not even complete strangers. (*Pause.*) You will be quite alone with your voice, there will be no other voice in the world but yours. (*Pause.*) Do you hear me?"

Though we hear a woman's voice from the loud-speaker, there is in fact no other voice in the world but Henry's. He is telling himself a story, vivid, particular, straining after compassion, the story of Bolton and Holloway, whose setting comes to us with entrancing particularity—

> Standing there in his old red dressinggown might go on fire any minute like when he was a child, no, that was his pyjamas, standing there waiting in the dark, no light, only the sound of the fire, and no sound of any kind, only the fire, an old man in great trouble.

This is more real than that chimerical sea. So is the snow-bound world through which Holloway comes: "Outside all still, not a sound, dog's chain maybe or a bough groaning if you stood there listening long enough." So the fictive world. The present world, on the contrary, is an occasion for delusions and testy imperatives ("Thuds, I want thuds! Like this!"), and the past world one for uncertain probing ("I can't remember if he met you." "You know he met me." "No, Ada, I don't know, I'm sorry, I have forgotten almost everything connected with you.") In his fictions however he moves with easy authority, since here at last everything will compose according to his whim, as Malone knew. But Henry's fiction culminates in an impasse, moving as it does to a situation like one Malone experienced in the flesh: a human encounter.

2

Malone, in bed, near death, records one evening an astonishing fact: "I have had a visit."

> I felt a violent blow on the head. He had perhaps been there for some time. One does not care to be kept waiting for ever, one draws attention to oneself as best one can, it's human. I don't doubt he gave me due warning, before he hit me. I don't know what he wanted. He's gone now. What an idea, all the same, to hit me on the head.

The blow on the head did not preface ampler communication. The visitor registered his presence, no more. "His mouth opened, his lips worked, but I heard nothing." Malone studied him at leisure, however; "He remained some time, seven hours at least." Later Malone draws up a written list of twenty-one questions, to be submitted if the man returns; but he does not. The list begins, "1. Who are you? 2. What do you do for a living? 3. Are you looking for something in particular? What else. 4. Why are you so cross? . . ." "Strange need," he notes, "to know who people are and what they do for a living and what they want with you."

Strange need, precisely; for how is the question, who are you, to be answered? Perhaps by a name. But let us say we know the name, Godot for instance. Who is Godot, what does he do for a living, and what does he want with Didi and Gogo? These are not really the things we want to know. Sometimes we know them. This man's name is Gaber, he makes his living as a courier of Youdi, and what he wants with Moran is to dispatch him after Molloy. Knowing this, what do we, or what does Moran, know of Gaber? If we idly assimilate his name to Gabriel's, and Youdi's to Yahweh, it is because we can think of nothing better to do, with the data supplied. Or let us have ampler data, a whole autobiography, such as Mercier and Camier were sluiced with in a southbound train:

> An only child I believe, I was born at P—. My parents were originally from Q—. From them it was that I received, along with the spirochete, the majestic nose whose ruins you behold. They were severe with me, but just. At the least deflection from rectitude my father beat me, with his heavy razor strop, until I bled, never failing however to notify my mother, so she could paint me with tincture of iodine or alcohol. Here doubtless is the explanation of my withdrawn and secretive character. . . .

. . . and so on for a thousand mortal words as old Madden rotates himself before our gaze; and from it we learn only this, that old Madden is a bore not *per accidens* but by predilection.

Whether cryptic or copious, talk in the Beckett universe is generally a mode of behavior, like Watt's oscillatory walk or Molloy's extraordinary performance with the sixteen stones. Sometimes, as when Pozzo demands undivided attention and sprays his throat with the vaporizer, it is highly studied behavior. But no more than the facial contortions of Malone's visitor ("his mouth opened, his lips worked, but I heard nothing") does it satisfy the "strange need." This is strangely jarring; we expect spoken words to reach, not merely gesticulate. But it conforms to the decorums of a writer whose sensibility, like Wordsworth's, explores the confines of a universe of objects, in which people are difficult to distinguish from apparitions, or else statistics. Wordsworth, it will be remembered, once on his wanderings encountered a Man whom in his account of the incident he likened successively to (a) a huge stone on a mountain top; (b) a sea beast crawled forth to sun itself; (c) a motionless cloud; and when the Man commenced to speak,

> his voice to me was like a stream
> Scarce heard; nor word from word could I divide;
> And the whole body of the Man did seem
> Like one whom I had met with in a dream.

Not otherwise did Molloy, for whom "to restore silence is the role of objects," observe that when another spoke, the words he heard, "and heard distinctly, having quite a sensitive ear, were heard a first time, then a second, and often even a third, as pure sounds, free of all meaning, and this is probably one of the reasons why conversation was unspeakably painful to me." Over his explanation of this phenomenon presides, we may say, Newton, of the prism and silent face: it was, thinks Molloy, "a defect of the understanding, perhaps, which only began to vibrate on repeated solicitations, or which did vibrate, if you like, but at a lower frequency, or a higher, than that of ratiocination, if such a thing is conceivable, and such a thing is conceivable, since I conceive it."

For Wordsworth is the optimistic poet, as Beckett is

the weeping comedian, of Newton's quiet machine. The statue in the Cambridge antechapel he recognized for what it was, a thing as silent as the face it represented, the marble index of a mind gone elsewhere, and meanwhile the very likeness of the entranced body. We do not fancy it about to speak; Newton is history's first unspeaking sage, his essential posture of operation summed up by a statue. Socrates in the bust is about to say something, or has just finished, but Newton has nothing to say. He engages in no Confucian or Socratic *viva voce* with disciples. His is something more than the normal mathematician's alogia; for we hear of Euclid teaching pupils, and Pythagoras sociably engaged with his brother cultists. He has no talk, he communes with a universe of objects, and makes note of results, each equation formally a tautology, which he is even negligent about publishing. He likened himself to a lone child gathering shells on the shore of the infinite ocean; so Molloy, "sitting on the shore, before the sea, the sixteen stones spread out before my eyes," meditates his problem of groups and cycles. And Wordsworth, having penetrated to the heart of Newton's romance as night after night starlight or moonlight drew his mind back to the statue in the antechapel, became in his turn in emulation of the Newtonian sage the Newtonian poet, the first poet to make a habit of wandering lonely as a cloud, among rocks, and stones and trees, encountering such things as lone thorns, banks of daffodils, mountains, and occasional human apparitions, lost so far as might be in his wise passiveness, indeed perpetually talking to himself "like a river murmuring" so that he was (he says so) grateful for the little dog that barked beside him when persons came near, and reminded him to restrain his mutterings and assume a social demeanor.[1] Through the social world, with which he feels no kinship, as through the world of objects, he moves as anomalously as an octopus in a forest; it is a universe for a clown. And he was the first to make a program of writing years afterward about his own experiences, and about himself in the process of writing about them, as Molloy and Moran and Malone do with such unflagging patience.

All Beckett protagonists enjoy an eerie kinship with earth's diurnal course: "I listen," writes Molloy, "and the voice is of a world collapsing endlessly, a frozen world, under a faint untroubled sky, enough to see by, yes, and frozen too." Again he participates in "the labour of the planet rolling eager into winter," and always he senses "these leaning things forever lapsing and crumbling away, beneath a sky without memory of morning or hope of night." It is in such passages that the sap flows; of encounters with persons Molloy is apt to report only his irritation. "All she asked was to feel me near her, with her," he reports of Mrs. Lousse's affecting entreaty; but "every now and then I interrupted her, to ask what town I was in." Later a charcoal burner exhibited the "strange need," and Molloy can only list it in a calculus of probabilities:

> I asked him to show me the nearest way out of the forest. I grew eloquent. His reply was exceedingly confused. Either I didn't understand a word he said, or he didn't understand a word I said, or he knew nothing, or he wanted to keep me near him. It was towards this fourth hypothesis that in all modesty I leaned, for when I made to go, he held me back by the sleeve. So I smartly freed

---

[1] See Book IV of *The Prelude*. In the next book he discloses his lifelong passion for Geometry, "an independent world, created out of pure intelligence."

a crutch and dealt him a good dint on the skull. That calmed him. The dirty old brute.

Show him a moon through his window, however, and impatience withers; he will move from observation—

> Two bars divided it into three segments, of which the middle remained constant, while little by little the right gained what the left lost—

to hypothesis—

> For the moon was moving from left to right, or the room was moving from right to left, or both together perhaps, or both were moving from left to right, but the room not so fast as the moon, or from right to left, but the moon not so fast as the room—

to poetry—

> And now its tranquil course was written on the walls, a radiance scored with shadow, then a brief quivering of leaves, if they were leaves, then that too went out, leaving me in the dark. . .

a pocket history of romanticism. Malone too feels for *things*, "notably little portable things of wood and stone," "and but for the company of these little objects which I picked up here and there, when out walking, and which sometimes gave me the impression that they too needed me, I might have been reduced to the society of nice people, or to the consolations of some religion or other, but I think not." He fondles them in his pockets, "as a way of talking to them and reassuring them," and when he discards them to make way for new loves, he is at pains to find "a place to lay them where they would be at peace forever, and no one ever find them short of extraordinary hazard, and such places are few and far between."

In this silent world, fount of the silence for which The Unnamable yearns, the silence held off by the go-on of his own voice yearning for it, in this world the great constants are physical laws: whether bits of natural lore ("Constipation is a sign of good health in pomeranians") or fanciful bits of efficient causality (Why do trains move off so smartly late at night? Why, because all along the line trainsmen are "anhelating toward their wives, after the long hours of continence"); or metaphors for a closed economy of emotion ("The tears of the world are a constant quantity. For each person who begins to weep somewhere else another stops. The same is true of the laugh.") or else a closed economy of effort and result (" . . . they would contrive things in such a way that I couldn't suspect the two vessels, the one to be emptied and the one to be filled, of being in reality one and the same . . . connected by pipes under the floor."). Murphy's friend Wylie applies the same analysis to private desire: "The syndrome known as life is too diffuse to admit of palliation. For every symptom that is eased, another is made worse. The horseleech's daughter[2] is a closed system. Her quantum of wantum cannot vary." It is a world locally freakish but totally shaped by two laws, the law of conservation of energy and the second law of thermodynamics. The former law states that nothing is added to or subtracted from the system, but simply mutated, and the latter states that the degree of organization within this closed system grows constantly less and so constantly less improbable, all actions being irreversible. The second law of thermodynamics is the real theme of Lucky's headlong oration, with its litany of labors "left unfinished for reasons unknown," its stream of elegiac phrases, "wastes and pines," "fades away," "the great

---

[2] "The horseleech hath two daughters, crying, Give, give.": Proverbs XXX-15. I owe this elucidation to an article by Mr. Samuel Mintz.

cold the great dark," "fading fading fading," and its computation to the nearest decimal of the dead loss per head since the death of Bishop Berkeley.

But this is insanity: several facts cry out against it. One is the extra hat that an unknown source injects into the system of *Waiting for Godot*, in defiance of law No. 1; and later we shall find the protagonist of *Comment C'est* agonizing over the boundless multiplication of sacks and sardine tins that destroys the closed system he has so painfully excogitated. Another affront to system is the dogged human will to keep on. A third is speech, which stubbornly will not remain "behavior."

In such a universe speech has no place; speech constantly threatens it with disruption. Sound, Descartes and Newton can account for, but speech defeats them. A voice reaching out of the interiority of a human person, with the thrust of my utter uniqueness, expressing, pressing out, so much as may be, toward some other person that sense of "I" which I alone have: what has Newton or Clerk Maxwell to say about that? So in Beckett's late dramatic work we find his cosmos dissociating into plays for voices alone, and "actes sans paroles." This dissociation exactly parallels that between thing and man. The second mime summarizes for the eye the physical universe à la *Molloy*: two men, never present to each other because one of them is always in a sack, alternately carrying one another ceaselessly to no end from right to left across a monolinear expanse of space. By contrast, the second radio play, *Embers*, summarizes for the ear the internal world from which reaches the unique voice:

> Stories, stories, years and years of stories, till the need came on me, for someone, to be with me, anyone, a stranger, to talk to, imagine he hears me, years of that, and then, now, for someone who . . . knew me, in the

old days, anyone, to be with me, imagine he hears me, what I am, now.

Put beside this a paragraph from *Watt*—

> Watt wore no tie, nor any collar. Had he had a collar, he would no doubt have found a tie, to go with it. And had he had a tie, he might perhaps have procured a collar, to carry it. But having neither tie, nor collar, he had neither collar, nor tie.

—and we see at once how this fine exercise in reciprocal negation and the anguish of Henry cannot coexist. Watt's tie and collar belong to the period of "Stories, stories, years and years of stories." That is where the Newtonian universe belongs also: it was a story Europe told itself for many decades. If Beckett's comedy derives from mathematics and system, from the impingement of system, and notably systematic forms of discourse, on experiences to which they seem inappropriate, it is to our quickening sense of persons imprisoned inside all this system that his works owe their grip on our attention. Persons stir because every word is an utterance. Patterns close because all discourse has shape.

The voice brings us to the mystery of the person, owes its very existence to that mystery, a mystery that, sour it and defile it as they will, no Beckett personage ever lays to rest. Krapp, in the most remarkable short dramatic piece in the language, communes with his own voice canned; what was once spoken in intimate urgent re-creation of experience—

> We drifted in among the flags and stuck. The way they went down, sighing, before the stem! (*Pause.*) I lay down across her with my face in her breasts and my hand on her. We lay there without moving. But under us all moved, and moved us, gently, up and down, and from side to side. . . .

—is thirty years later reproduced exactly, and again, and yet again, with precise automatic repetition of nuance, false as three traced signatures: not a voice any more but a hideously exact simulacrum of a voice, on magnetic tape: recollection in tranquillity with an automaton's vengeance: a last bitter parody of those vases celebrated in *Proust*, where the lost past is sealed away. We can see why the author of *Mercier et Camier* and the trilogy expresses a recurrent interest in parrots.

"Bless you Willie . . . ," says Winnie in *Happy Days*,

> . . . just to know that in theory you can hear me even though in fact you don't is all I need, just to feel you there within earshot and conceivably on the qui vive is all I ask. . .

for otherwise,

> . . . what would I do what *could* I do, all day long, I mean between the bell for waking and the bell for sleep? (*Pause.*) Simply gaze before me with compressed lips.

For it is inconceivable that speech should not reach toward another person, and when late in the play it seems at last advisable that she should come to terms with this possibility (". . . it is a long time now, Willie, since I saw you."), it remains inconceivable.

> I used to think . . . (*Pause.*) . . . I say I used to think that I would learn to talk alone. (*Pause.*) By that I mean to myself, the wilderness. (*Smile.*) But no. (*Smile broader.*) No no. (*Smile off.*) Ergo you are there."

Bring, then, persons into juxtaposition, and perhaps by some miracle the locked selves will flower. The whole tension of *Waiting for Godot* depends on this possibility; for Godot being a person and not a physical law, will introduce into the repetitive universe of Didi and Gogo some unpredictable disposition of their affairs: "Let's wait and see what he says." And we see why *Mercier et Camier* fritters into aimlessness, the object of the quest being merely a bicycle. Godot is the perpetual possibility of personal impingement on mechanism; without him, their interrelation, from long habit, has become a shuffling of limited resources, their conversation a game of catch ("Come on, Gogo, return the ball, can't you, once in a way?"), their choice either submitting to protracted existence or terminating it. Godot does not come, but his perpetual possibility animates the weary trickle of potency into history.

Bring, then, persons into juxtaposition, and perhaps . . . *Embers* does so bring them, in Henry's fantasy, and fiction stops dead at a terrible, poignant climax. Bolton, in the story Henry tells to himself, has summoned Dr. Holloway in the dead of night, and when Holloway arrives can only fix his eye and say in anguish, "Please! PLEASE!" The scene is intensely vivid. All Henry's dormant human capacity flows into his evocation of the "old man in great trouble," of Holloway coming to him through a nearly interplanetary silence. ("Outside all still, not a sound, dog's chain maybe or a bough groaning if you stood there listening long enough, white world, Holloway with his little black bag, not a sound, bitter cold, full moon small and white, crooked trail of Holloway's galoshes, Vega in the Lyre very green.") They stand in each other's presence, and all that Henry wanted from the father who despised him and the wife he despised suddenly animates a haunting tableau: Bolton asking mutely for what cannot be specified, for whatever communion looks out of another's eyes.

> Then he suddenly strikes a match, Bolton does, lights a candle, catches it up above his head, walks over and looks Holloway full in the eye. (*Pause.*) Not a word, just a

look, the old blue eye, very glassy, lids worn thin, lashes gone, whole thing swimming, and the candle shaking over his head. . . . "We've had this before, Bolton, don't ask me to go through it again." (*Pause.*) Bolton: "Please!" (*Pause.*) "Please!" (*Pause.*) "Please, Holloway!" (*Pause.*) Candle shaking and guttering all over the place, lower now, old arm tired, [with what sympathy Henry's affections invade the old man of his fantasy!] takes it in the other hand and holds it high again, that's it, that was always it, night, and the embers cold, and the glim shaking in your old fist, saying, Please! Please! (*Pause.*) Begging. (*Pause.*) Of the poor.

Holloway covers his face: "Not a sound, white world, bitter cold, ghastly scene, old men, great trouble, no good."

Their great trouble is that they are each of them alone; out of all his intimate sense of his own identity, which no one else can ever share, comes Bolton's "Please!" across the bitter gulf: the distillation of the recurrent Beckett scene in which two men are brought into each other's presence and merely look at each other.

3

Or merely listen to each other—Krapp and the vanished Krapp imprisoned on the tape; or merely badger each other—Victor and the committee of interrogators in *Eleutheria*; or engage in reciprocal tyranny—Hamm and Clov. Or else one, awaited, does not come (Godot); or one, sought, is not there (Murphy, Molloy); or one, there, cannot cease to be (The Unnamable). The Beckett tension is between the person and the mathematical zero; hence his preoccupation with series and permutation, with the unique tenacities of declarative syntax, which so order and encase mute agonies, and with silence. The Beckett plot is simply an encounter between persons: hence the journeyings, the waitings, the confrontations.

And the resolution of the Beckett plot? Either an infinite series, or else an impasse.

His mathematical world is at bottom utterly frustrating, because it cannot assimilate persons and I am a person. His people never cease to court this frustration, because the mind once endowed with an orderly language and with the principles of logic can function in no other way. Yet no system for selecting the sucking stones can fully appease Molloy's fierce appetite for order. ("But I was tired, but I was tired, and I contented myself ingloriously with the first solution that was a solution, to this problem.") No sequence of sentences can approximate the ultimate statement The Unnamable yearns to make, since every sentence must begin somewhere and end somewhere else (*abitus, transitus, aditus,* wrote Geulincx) and no choice of a beginning or an ending can fail to exclude a thousand others. Though his sentences grow longer as tension mounts (the first has two words, the last some 1,700), yet each having chosen its terminus and direction can incorporate no others. And the Lynch family, surely Beckett's most grotesque comic invention, strives in vain to bring its combined ages to 1,000 years; breed though it will, peopling the land with hemophiliacs, idiots, paralytics, and other human variants, it cannot hope that even twins each aged four months can offset the loss of three brothers aged sixty-five, sixty-sixty-four and sixty-three. The great numbers perish while the numerous small ones wax, man's days being limited; and there seems little likelihood of the millenium ever being brought nearer than the eight and a half months that remained just before four deaths rolled back the total by a hopeless seventeen years.

A person cannot be silent, even voyaging through strange seas of thought; there is no interior silence. Nor alone, since we cannot imagine what it is not to be with oneself. Not even by retreating so far as may be within himself can he escape confrontation with the Other, since his very words shape alternate persons, his very musings subdivide himself. Not even by resigning himself, with Molloy, to "senseless, speechless, issueless misery" can he evade the symmetries and permutations that torment the mind.

Oneself, another person, symmetries, tensions: more than a dozen years after the trilogy *Comment C'est*, an unexpected return to fiction, gave these themes their strangest, most abstract and most hauntingly intimate development. Built phrase by phrase into a beautifully and tightly wrought structure, a few dozen expressions permuted with deliberate redundancy accumulate meaning even as they are emptied of it, and offer themselves as points of radiation in a strange web of utter illusion. For this book is founded on nothing recognizable; compared to it even the trilogy is realistic narrative. It is built out of little more than a basic French vocabulary and a stock of phrases, and built before our eyes, employing writing as a metaphor for itself much as *Endgame* employs the stage, calculating the amount of work still ahead, admitting ill-judged phrases with an abstracted "quelquechose là qui ne va pas," and finishing with relief ("bon bon fin de la troisième partie et dernière"). It evades *The Unnamable*'s difficulties with the sentence by employing none. So thoroughly does syntax give way to rhythm and architecture that we acquiesce without discomfort to the total absence of punctuation. In Molly Bloom's monologue the commas and full stops are merely left out. By contrast it is the mark of Beckett's fierce purity that he makes all thought of them seem irrelevant. The three full stops on these 177 pages are presumably printer's inadvertencies. The book looks like a draft of itself, as *Endgame* feels like a rehearsal of itself; packets of language, set apart by spaces, like notes for paragraphs never to be composed, jotted as some eternal voice dictates ("I say it as I hear it"):

> voice once without quaqua on all sides then in me when I stop panting now in me tell me again finish telling me invocation . . .

> my life last state last version ill said ill heard ill recaptured when the panting stops ill murmured to the mud brief movements of the lower face losses everywhere

From the first words we feel as never before the tension of an alien person:

> how it was I quote before Pim with Pim after Pim how it is part one part two part three I say it as I hear it

Part One is animated throughout by the thought of Pim, whose name occurs in it some fifty times, nearly always as the object of some preposition. Before Pim, with Pim, after Pim; toward Pim, near Pim; the words of Pim, the watch of Pim: these categories sketch a domain of being, of moving, and of knowing in which Pim, Beckett's generic other person, is the stable and ordering principle. Pim confers, it seems, all the meaning that the life before us can aspire to. In the absence of his name, acrid memories circulate without point, small mean words buzz, and we are reduced to such calming expedients as the drawing of the free hand over the face ("that's a help when all fails food for thought"). This, we are given to understand, is "how it was before Pim," and the substance of Part One is the journey toward Pim, a dogged chronicle of slogging through mud: "vast stretch of time when I drag myself and drag myself amazed that I can the cord sawing my neck the sack jolting at my side a hand outstretched

towards the wall the ditch that never come." This journey is over and now being recapitulated; yet as we follow
the narrative, which is generally in the present tense ("I
shall never have any past never had"), Pim lies ahead.
To these facts the reader finds himself paying little attention, so true are they of all fiction. Beckett has paid close
attention, however, and out of the consequent identifica-
tion of Pim past with Pim future he will spin before the
book is finished an infinite series. This possibility the
reader of the first part is unlikely to notice, despite ample
clues; we suppose therefore that our sojourn in this bleak
time will be redeemed by the person so many allusions
promise, and that the minimal assets of this bleak place
(mud, a jute sack, tinned fish, a can opener, a cord) will
assume the proper insignificance of all mere things when
Pim is present at last.

It is legitimate meanwhile to wonder where we are.
Though "la boue" may vaguely recall the place "in the
Marne mud" where Beckett moved his belongings by
wheelbarrow during the hungry winter of 1947, and
where nine years later he wrote *Fin de Partie*, this information is whimsically extraneous to the present book,
the uncertainties of which are not of a geographical
order. Mud, darkness, and an indefinite sense of distance
determine the ambience. Molloy recalled how "the road,
hard and white, seared the tender pastures, rose and fell
at the whim of hills and hollows," but no such order of
experience is in question here. Such precisions belong to
a former life, "up there in the light," where others, it
seems, still move, doubtless like the folk Malone envis-
aged, "their great balls and sockets rattling and clack-
ing like knackers, each on his way." But here there is no
light, nor no speech except soundless "brief movements
of the lower face," nor no walking apparently, since all is

a dragging and crawling ("ten yards fifteen yards half on my left side right foot right hand push pull flat on my belly mute cries half on my right side left foot left hand push pull flat on my belly mute cries not a syllable to be changed in this description"). It is a sort of limbo, one supposes, or a sort of hell. Toward the end of the journey even the sack is lost, with all its contents.

Will Pim brighten the world? No, the sojourn with Pim is distressing beyond expectation. Not a total loss, though:

> happy period in its way part two I speak of part two with Pim how it was good moments good for me I speak of me good for him too I speak of him too happy too in his way I shall know it later I shall know his way of happiness I shall have it I have not yet had everything

Pim's happiness consists chiefly in this, that but for my coming he would be "nothing but a carcass inert and mute forever flat in the mud." His existence as Pim, his very name, depends on my presence. He lies spreadeagled face down throughout our séance, clutching a sack of his own, but from the moment of my arrival commences to emit articulate sounds into the mud, though my efforts to speak are restricted as before to "brief movements of the lower face." Having ascertained by groping which end of him is which ("the cries tell me which end is his head but I could be mistaken"), I take up my position "in the dark the mud my head against his my side pressed against his my right arm around his shoulders he cries no more we rest thus a good while there are good whiles." And what is transacted during our "vie en commun" is first, an incomprehensible song by Pim, in a foreign tongue perhaps, and then a series of startling cruelties.

For a moment the voice of Pim ("a human voice there a

few inches away my dream") seemed to promise more
generous intimacies:

> one day we should set forth again together . . . help one
> another forward fall down in unison and lie there in
> each other's arms till it be time to go on

—but without explanations the will of this place supervenes; they commence the game of tyrant and victim, that
familiar Beckett coupling, like Hamm and Clov, Moran
and his son, Pozzo and Lucky, even a little Didi and Gogo.
Clov, Lucky, Moran *fils*, are well trained, and pedagogical
method is now demonstrated. Clawed beneath the right
arm Pim repeatedly utters cries which blows on the
skull repeatedly stifle in facefuls of mud; until after aeons
of time of being clawed he chances to sing instead of
crying, and is encouraged by a blow withheld to interpret
the clawed armpit as a command to sing ("question of
training"). Next the can opener is jabbed into his rump
until he learns ("not stupid merely slow") that this is
the signal to speak. These ritual lessons occupy vast tracts
of time, and the author does not omit to tabulate the cur-
riculum of stimuli:

> one sing nails in the armpit two speak blade of canopener
> in the rump three stop thump on the skull four louder
> handle of canopener in the kidney

> five softer index in the anus six bravo slap athwart
> the buttocks seven bad same as three eight again same
> as one or two as needed

All this is executed neither in sorrow nor in anger, but
with an analytic fulness of participation on which many
pages are expended.

Once trained, Pim can be conversed with. The mute
narrator sustains his part with fist, can opener and nails,
in a last refinement tracing written questions on Pim's

back ("roman capitals from left to right and from top to bottom as in our civilization": two Chinamen would have observed a different convention). And Pim for his part murmurs responses, having to do with his life "up there in the light." His life merges with mine, his voice with my muteness; it is unclear to whom the memories belong.

> that alleged life then he had had invented remembered a little of each no knowing that thing up above he gave it to me I made it mine what I fancied skies especially roads especially . . .

It is the narrator who claims the most vivid and affecting memories, of a lost wife, Pam Prim, whom he can barely bring himself to think about. She terminated, for him, an energetic career ("tried everything building especially was flourishing all branches especially plaster met Pam I believe"). Their intimacy was brief:

> love birth of love increase decrease death efforts to revive through the anus joint vain through the cunt again vain again out of the window threw herself or fell back broken hospital daisies.

Her death in the hospital, forgiving him (for what?), his visits there, sitting on her bed holding before her face the flowers she could not turn her head to see; his walk away from the place, "winter icy road black branches grey with rime she up there at the top dying forgiving all white" —these memories he retraces as Henry in *Embers* does his life with Ada, or causes Pim to recite as Krapp plays again and again the tape which embalms his gone passion. Pim is by turns a Lucky to keep company with and abuse, a Krapp's record of one's own past, shifted out of one's mind into another less painful location, and an intimate self telling stories as Henry tells himself stories. Like the tape he can be switched on and off by the application of stimuli two and three; like oneself, he murmurs with a creative intimacy Krapp's machine cannot approximate; like Lucky, Moran *fils*, or Clov he is a person, inalienably other, filling a need, capable even of evoking present affection ("arm around his poor shoulders rest we've earned it"). He is plied, after these memories, with a fusillade of questions to which he answers yes and no without imparting much enlightenment; and at length is there no more. So much for Pim.

So much, at present, for Pim. That was how the encounter turned out. But, we are given to understand, it always turns out that way, and the narrator neither exults in his own cruelty nor regrets it. For in Part Three he is awaiting in his turn a certain Bom, who will serve him, and has served him before, as he served Pim, after which he will commence the journey to Pim again. Pim, while he waits, is now journeying through the mud to torment another. Now, as he waits himself to play the Pim, having in Part Two played the Bom ("it's our justice"), he reflects on the logistics of the operation: first of the sacks, of which during an infinite number of journeys an infinite number are found, exchanged, permuted, and lost according to a rule as elaborate as the one that governed Molloy's sucking stones: then of the personnel, of whom any number are thinkable, exchanging in sets of four the roles of *bourreau* and *victime*, but each having to do with only two others, the one ahead of him on the route, whom he catches up to and torments, the one behind him who catches up to him and torments him. At intervals half are waiting, half are moving; at alternate intervals, the couples are about their solemn business. For allied reasons, he notes, a three-part book gives an adequate sample, for the invariable rhythm which obtains in this place ("our justice demands it") is journey, torture, wait, be tortured, but phase four repeats phase two so exactly that we can dispense with another torture piece.

Yet it was not wholly a torture piece, despite the can opener: they shared food, memories and the sensation of existing: "more lively there's nothing better." Deprived of Pim we calculate and speculate, alone with the implacable stammering voice, perhaps my own ("I say it as I hear it"). We may guess, indeed, that the risk of this three-part account being incomplete, omitting "a thousand things little visible or not at all in the present version," is negligible, so total was the sharing.

> the small need of a life of a voice on the part of one who has neither

> the voice extorted a few words life because of cry that proves it in deep with the blade that's all is needed a little cry all is not dead we drink we give to drink good-bye

> they were I quote good moments yes somehow good moments when you think

> Pim and I part two and Bom and I part four what that will be when you think

> to say after that we knew each other even then

> cleaved together two bodies one in the dark the mud

> motionless but for the right arm brief flurry now and then all the needful

> to say after that that I knew Pim that Pim knew me and Bom and I that we'll know each another even for a moment

But sharing, as he pursues his thoughts, ceases to be one of his terms of reference; he grows preoccupied again with questions of symmetry, of literary tactics (how comes this written account of a place where one lies flat in the mud? Why, one Kram, not one of us, writes down my words in his notebook and then mounts back into the light) ; and questions, once again, of logistics. For the sacks are a puzzle. As he tries explanation after explanation he sounds more and more like a writer trying to salvage a considerable quantity of work in which he has found, too late, a logical flaw. For the whole unimaginable procession moves on a narrow track eastward (as in *Mime II* the two men with sacks are steadily goaded from stage left to stage right), and as each starts a new journey he must find a sack of provisions. But if all the sacks have been in place from eternity then at each place where a sack is to be found there must be an infinite number to provide for the infinite number of travelers each of whom will halt there: whence, total blockage from the outset:

> such a mountain of sacks at the very setting forth that all progress impossible and no sooner imparted to the caravan its unthinkable first impulsion than it at a standstill for ever and frozen in injustice

> then from left to right or west to east the atrocious spectacle on into the black night of future time of a tormentor abandoned who will never be tormented then a little space then his brief journey over prone at the foot of a mountain of victuals the tormented who will never be tormentor then a great space then another abandoned and so on infinitely

In which case, we perceive in this vertigo of ratiocination, every segment of the route would be blocked, and equally, by the same reasoning, our justice. There seems nothing for it but to postulate a superior being who sees to the supply of sacks as they are needed; and he is just putting the finishing touches to the theology and eschatology of this new hypothesis, when the *peripeteia* of the book is suddenly sprung.

For it is simplest to suppose that no component of the problem which has been occupying him for sixty pages has any existence, that he has been telling himself a story, and that the voice whose words he has been re- peating ("I say it as I hear it") has been his own. No Pim then, no Bom, no journey, no sack. He tries this out catechetically, and the voice (his own?) agrees:

> all these calculations yes explanations yes the whole story from one end to the other yes completely false yes

Nothing, in this case, is real but the mud and the black- ness. Even the higher being, the source of the voice and perhaps of the sacks, disappears; even Samuel Beckett, for that matter, disappears:

> but these stories of voices yes quaqua yes of other worlds yes of someone in another world yes whose dreams so to speak I am yes which he dreams all the time yes tells all the time yes his only dream yes his only story yes . . .

> and these stories of up above yes the light yes the skies yes a little blue yes a little white yes the turning earth yes bright and less bright yes little scenes yes all balls yes the women yes the dog yes the prayers the homes yes all balls yes

But almost the final words are "end of quotation": this solipsism may be a final delusion imparted by the voice, and to imagine that he is merely telling himself a story may be (there is no way to tell, unless he can tell whether the voice is his own) a delusion that comes on schedule while one waits for Bom. At any rate,

> good good end of the third and last part there it is that's how it was end of quotation after Pim how it is

So the work closes, balanced on a knife edge; and so Beck- ett rounds off in a perfectly insoluble either-or this fullest and most philosophical summary of "the dream yes which he dreams all the time yes tells all the time yes his only dream yes his only story yes."

4

This work contains no ingredient (unless perhaps mud) which we have not encountered before. What is new is the absolute sureness of design. We have had sacks in the second mime, crawling in *Molloy*, a horizontal narrator in *Malone Dies*, pages of broken tentative utterance in *Embers*, tyrant and victim repeatedly, stories told to oneself repeatedly, lost love in *Krapp's Last Tape*, a voice quaqua disturbing limbo in *The Unnamable*, agonies of non-identity in the *Textes Pour Rien*. The blind Hamm and the blind Mr. Rooney were at rest and in motion respectively in an utter darkness, and the latter is also enamored of computations ("Not count! One of the few satisfactions in life?") Even the technique of communicating by a code of blows was adumbrated by Molloy, seeking to impress "one knock yes, two no, three I don't know, four money, five goodbye" on his mother's "ruined and frantic understanding." Everything, moreover, that Beckett has written from *Murphy* onward shows us persons who once were alive in the bright world and have somehow ceased to be so. Murphy never thinks of doubting that he has been fortunate to die into the little chaos within, but no one after him is quite so sure. Paradise in any case, if there ever was one, has been lost, and the subtle argument of *Proust*, that only involuntary memory can briefly restore it, is exactly borne out when Pim helps us recall what without him we cannot reach, the vanished days. It is even true, as we were told it would be in *Proust*, that the attempt to communicate where no communication is possible is "horribly comic," exactly the phrase for the business with fist and can opener.

No, what is novel is simply the scale on which this material is organized, the brilliance no longer local but gone into the bones of a work that tends to stay in the memory as a whole. Not that it hangs there like a static pattern fleshed out: it is a process, a history of effort, the heroic effort to get itself written. The narrator, unlike even The Unnamable, is doing without pencil and paper (how would he even see his notes?), and as he addresses himself to the more intricate calculations of Part Three we watch him assembling and reassembling, by dint of repetition, the data in his memory with the awe we should bring to the spectacle of a Newton born blind. We do not expect sentences, they would be an irrelevant elegance.

And that the master of syntax should have chosen to do without the sentence, even this is not surprising when we recall his thematic distrust of accomplishment. It was almost the last thing left for him to discard from his repertory, and he gained in discarding it a structural wholeness, as of a cantilever bridge, only to be achieved by getting rid of all those little beginnings and endings. Repeatedly similar components intersect at similar angles, like girders, and it is with relief, not annoyance, that we encounter repeatedly like an old friend some tried formulation, "jambe droite bras droit pousse tire dix mètres quinze mètres": a relief we share with the narrator, who for some instants is spared the necessity of invention.

Our author is indomitable, like Pim singing. Wedged in this crack, where the very names are provisional, and without so much as a declarative sentence to call his own, he excogitates a whole grotesque vision of judgment, on the scale of a lesser Dante, with greater authority than when he had all the resources of fiction at his dis-

posal and wrote the tale of Murphy and his friends, "là-
haut dans la lumiére." It is at last, to paraphrase the dialogue
written eleven years earlier, the situation of him who is
helpless, cannot act, in the end cannot write, since he is
obliged to write; the act of him who, helpless, unable to
act, acts, in the end writes, since he is obliged to write.
(Why is he obliged to write? I don't know. Why is he helpless to write? Because there is nothing to write and nothing
to write with.) He has always told the same story; the memories of the road outside the hospital where Pam Prim died
reach all the way back to a poem in *Echo's Bones*:

> Exeo in a spasm
> tired of my darling's red sputum
> from the Portobello Private Nursing Home . . .

We might even, with all the books and tales before us,
arrange the story into a chronolgy. A man (first version)
is thrown out of the house by his upright family ("L'Expulsé") , and slowly loses the capacity for human intercourse; or (second version) is so shocked by the gratuitous death of a loved one that he slowly loses the capacity
for human intercourse; wanders for some years on the
continent and in London (*Murphy*), puzzling over the
realities of the Irish world in which he once participated
(*Watt*) ; has for a while a companion (*Mercier et Camier*)
with whom, having become a twilight man, he is never
able to achieve a satisfactory intimacy; rediscovers a need
for his mother (*Molloy*) but does not prosecute it;
lapses into telling himself endless stories (*Malone Dies*)
and so into an inferno of words (*The Unnamable*) in
which the last shreds of his identity dissolve; then stirred
at last by a hunger he has never admitted (*Godot, Embers*) for the presence and succor of other persons, some
other person, excogitates out of his now irremediable
darkness (*Comment C'est*) a myth of his hopeless situa-

tion and a fiction of what release into memory another
presence might bring to it. This coheres agreeably and
will very likely some day be the theme of some biographer
or other. We should recall how Moran commenced his
narrative:

> Then I went back into the house and wrote, It is mid-
> night. The rain is beating on the windows. It was not
> midnight. It was not raining.

—and reflect that there is likely not an atom of truth in
these conjectures from start to finish. We have been
cunningly closed up in a huge fantasy; and if anyone is
tempted to see behind blind Hamm the figure, say, of
James Joyce exacting minute services of a disciple, it is
sufficient to note that Malone's tale touches Malone's life
at many points without its eerie abundance of invention
being thereby explained. Fiction is precisely like mathematics in this, that its normal processes handle nonexis-
tent beings (points without magnitude, lines without
breadth, persons without being), and that a knowing
extension of its normal processes will generate beings
that cannot be assimilated by the world of experience.
The surds and the imaginary numbers are irrefutable
productions of a system that finds it has no place for
them.

Beckett's work, in the same way, is far from being a
by-product of hopeless misery. It is the unassimilable
product of a set of operations with words, every word of
which retains its meaning and every operation its validity.
And the work leaps from end to end with comic invention. The population of the world being reduced to four,
concern is expressed about the absence of bicycle wheels.
A man sits on nothing identifiable, in a gray space, while
a figment of his past invention rotates about him, its
two hands propping up its jaw. Twenty-eight people

yearn day and night for the morning when their combined ages will total 1,000 years. The whole world crawls
from left to right along an invisible track, subsisting on
tinned fish. Or, in a longer perspective, certain general
propositions. Item: the universe is a congeries of largely
random phenomena, amid which however we can discern
certain tokens of stability; these are, bowler hats, bicycles,
the letter M. Item: what I am telling you is a story, the
substance of which is that it is a story; now since my
statement that these facts are fiction is part of the fiction,
they may very likely be facts, but if they are facts then
you are to believe what they say, namely that they are
fictions. (Was it or was it not raining when Moran began to write? For his statement that it was not is contained in the lie which it is the point of the statement to
expose as a lie). This last antinomy was known to our
fathers as the paradox of the Cretan liar: all Cretans are
liars, said the man from Crete. It exercised logic classrooms
for centuries.

And indeed Beckett's fictions are at bottom rather like
scholarly jokes. It is in the classroom that such mad
worlds are postulated, as it is there that a hapless candi-
date is hauled before examiners and bidden, like Lucky,
to take off his hat and think. A, B, and C must fill a water
butt. A carries his water twice as far as B and C but walks
three times as fast. C's bucket leaks half its contents during an average journey. Express as a ratio their relative
frustrations. A textbook prepared about 1835 for the use
of the Irish National Schools[3] invites us to "detain the
earth a moment at point D" while we perform a small
calculation, and directing our attention to a common

---

[3] I owe this analogy to Professor Donald Pearce. Being compiled from
miscellaneous sources, the book gives a good cross section of academe's
obtuse explicitness.

table, reminds us that were the cohesion "so far destroyed as to convert the wood into a fluid, no support could be afforded by the legs; for the particles no longer cohering together [formulation in its lunacy must pursue the uttermost particles of the obvious], each would press separately and independently, and would be brought to a level with the surface of the earth." This was written a century before Dali. Only pedagogy would convert table legs into water, or solemnly doubt that there is less land in the southern hemisphere than in the northern ("for it is possible that the land may be only rather depressed in the south, and consequently covered by the sea"); or elaborate, with reasons, the truth that vegetables have no stomach; or reflect that whereas a dead body soon begins to putrefy, until nothing remains but dust, "this never happens in life." Even so Malone noted that when you roll over, the head comes to rest x inches from where it was before, x being the width of the shoulders in inches; and Molloy, that a certain inconceivable thing was indeed conceivable since he conceived it.

For Beckett is the first great academic clown since Sterne. If *Comment C'est* (a title for any realistic novel whatever) is from one point of view a grave and mordant image for the lot of man, from another it is like a non-Euclidean geometry, the elaboration of a fantastic premise. All his fictions of the minimal and the deprived, presenting men as less than they are, petty, consistent, stubbornly obsessed, answer rigorously to the conditions of comedy prescribed by Aristotle, the schoolmaster of Europe. His gentle allusive jokes recall those of a schoolmaster who has lived much by himself, a role he knows well how to play. He is never far from the academic *blagueur*, whether indulging his striking talent for exposition (Molloy on the sucking stones becomes in effect

a lecture-demonstration), or recalling the conditions under which he learned his French as a single verb in several
moods or tenses generates the kind of pointlessly heated
vignette with which language textbooks are sprinkled, or
casually fondling the problem by which Clov is too tired
to be exercised, at what instant, as grains of sand trickle
onto a given spot, we may be said to have a heap. And
we may remember with what loving care he shaped the
story of Louit, who located a man named Tisler who
lived in a room on the canal, and passed off this man, did
Louit, before a five-man examining committee as an un-
lettered rustic capable of the mental extraction of cube
roots and so of illustrating The Mathematical Intuitions
of the Visicelts. Ever and ever evoking the French classes
and mathematics classes where his mind was formed, he
plays ever bleaker homage to the fact that ours is a classroom civilization, and that schoolmasters are the un-
acknowledged legislators of the race. Each of his bums
has at some far off time been well schooled, "up there in
the light," furnished with words and processes, facts and
analogies. They have read Geulincx in the Latin, they
savor recurring decimals and the laws of permutation, the
West has discharged upon them the fulness of its in-
structional method, and look at them.

Spinning, with a look of foxy innocence, his fantasies of
language, mathematics, and logic, fastidious in his low
bohemia, evading the nets with which we catch men of
letters (no more to tell us than Molloy had to tell the
policeman; blank on every pertinent topic), and looking
at us out of photographs as though calculating his
chances of being given a loaf of bread, this learned vagrant moves through the rigors of today's world like a
ghost from the middle ages, as scandalously elusive as the

twelfth-century archpoet who "weeping left the country of the laughing" and composed, no one knows when or where, the song beginning

> Estuans intrinsecus
> ira vehementi
> in amaritudine
> loquar meae menti.

And living as we do amid moving toys and vociferous unrealities, shaken by every assault on our beliefs, on our orientation in the world ("I have forgotten which way I am facing." "You have turned aside and are bowed down over the ditch."), on our very identities; acquiescing as abstractions challenge customs, multitudinous data puzzle the will, and an acerb indifference muffles our natures, we quiver as his fantasies of displacement and non-being strike our nerves, half ready to believe (as we draw back) that we indeed wander in a forest, that our intellection permutes stones, that we do no more than tell ourselves tales while we die, or drag our possessions along with us in sacks.

In our fascinated affinity with these twilight men, none of them visible to the eyes with which we pursue our affairs (and what are our affairs?) we barely credit the ritual disavowal—

> never any procession no nor journey no never any Pim no nor Bom no never anyone no but me no answer but me yes . . .

—and barely notice how cunningly it does not disavow. Yes, yes, I am mistaken, I am mistaken, said B. in the same way, to placate D. These books do not undo the world; it will be here tomorrow. The fascination remains, with the permanence of all ordered things. And the books are fictions. There is only ourselves, disturbed but obscurely appeased, and the scholar vagrant, comedian of the impasse, aloof, unassimilable, shy.

Santa Barbara, California
1961

In the six years since this book was finished, Beckett has published one long work, *How It Is* (being *Comment C'est* so completely rethought in English that "translated" seems an inapplicable word) , and completed some nine short works for various media which explore an aesthetic of ultra-compression. Having nothing new to say about *How It Is,* I have let the translated excerpts from *Comment C'est* stand in my text, though they no longer represent Beckett's final English equivalents. Two French short stories, *Assez* and *Bing* (both 1966) , I content myself with commending to the reader. But the short dramatic works for radio, television, film, and stage define a new departure sufficiently teasing to justify a supplementary chapter, which begins overleaf.

January 1967

H. K.

Progress Report, 1962-1965

1

Beckett's way of making progress is like that of the man in *How It Is*—"ten yards fifteen yards semi-side left right leg right arm push pull flat on face imprecations no sound"—varying nothing except the program of mute imprecations and dragging after him everything he has had since he started. That is why, as his works multiply, their resemblances become more and more striking, for their components, it grows increasingly clear, are drawn from a limited set. It is also why their originality grows more and more absolute, devising new sets of rules by which the familiar pieces may be chosen and shown. To play one more game by the old rules would be merely competence, and a new medium (film, television) is a great liberator of invention. Inspecting, therefore, the stage plays since *Endgame* (*Happy Days* and *Play*) or the radio plays since *Embers* (*Words and Music* and *Cascando*) or the film (*Film*) or the TV play (*Eh Joe*), or even the fictional fragment (*Imagination Dead Imagine*), we sense with equal accuracy that we have seen all their elements before, and that the author nevertheless is repeating nothing. And one last little play, the "dramaticule" *Come and Go*, in evading most of the familiar Beckett rituals contrives to be the most characteristic of all.

All these works are mysteriously situated, in that never-world which is perhaps the interior of the author's head, or the auditor's. Their action (except for that of *Come and Go*) proceeds at the bidding of some mysterious authority which resembles Murphy's "process of supernatural determination," so that the figures before us perform but do not design their performance.

209

This authority is itself one of the figures before us, in the acoustical space of the radio plays where it is so difficult to give a meaning to "before us": the inciting croaking voice in *Words and Music,* the voice of the "Opener" ("dry as dust" but frantic later) in *Cascando.* In the visual works, betrayed by no tremor because inaudible, it expresses its will more austerely, the eye's being the rhetoric of tyranny as the ear's of misgivings. It distils the authority of the very medium: the TV camera itself, the ciné camera itself. In *Play* it directs the inquisitorial spotlight, in *Happy Days* it rings "the bell for waking and the bell for sleep."

These bells, according to the convention of *Happy Days,* are indispensable, daylight being now eternal. Yet mechanical though they are, they cannot counterfeit the indifference with which a turning earth's daylight comes and goes; somebody is ringing them, and what they mechanize remains vestigially a voice. If Winnie does not at once begin her day, the waking bell rings again, "more piercingly." "Someone is looking at me still," she reflects as its echoes die out. "Caring for me still. (*Pause.*) That is what I find so wonderful. (*Pause.*) Eyes on my eyes. (*Pause.*)" If she knew she was in a theater we might suppose she was speaking of the audience, whose presence exacts her performance, and thanks to whose interest the run of the play continues, as she sinks deeper into the rote of her part, gesturing at last with nothing more than her eyes. It is like Beckett to contrive as bleak a play as possible, and then toy with the fancy of its running interminably; equally like him to work so close to the nerve of the form that we cannot tell whether our own remorseless curiosity is part of the play or not. Perhaps it is not; the bell, though it synchronizes with our impatience, would be rung by the stage electrician with equal rigor were the opening-night house empty. It resembles in this way the will of God, which commands the private as surely as the public self. The importunate flickering spotlight that directs the human orchestra of *Play* is in the same way both a metaphor for our attention (relentless, all-consuming, whimsical) and a force within the play which *directs* our attention, and on which we rely for direction, as moviegoers rely on the camera. A play is an inquisition at which we connive. Once it has ceased to resemble the *Oresteia* or even *Richard II*, a public ritual religious in context, a play transforms itself into a low ritual of curiosity, the symbols of which are not the hero and his fate, but the curtain, the cues, the lights. The drama of Ibsen and his successors celebrates our conviction that we have a right to *find out*. Blending deceptively with the unknown world, it reduces the known world, people and all, to the plane where specimens are studied. A meanness sours the cosmos of all these late works; and it is our own.

Endgame was Beckett's one homage to the drama of Sophocles and Shakespeare: an x-ray version of the heroic play, dominated by Hamm, a prince of players. Its predecessor, *Waiting for Godot*, reflected something more primitive; the intercourse of clowns, before the arrival of a hero who does not arrive. *Happy Days* with its plethora of domestic detail, is post-heroic: toothbrush, lipstick, shopping-bag, parasol, and a great fat heroine who sings and smiles and quotes and projects her battered personality: her things are the bric-a-brac and hers the rituals of an English music-hall "turn," circa 1910. Already the compassion of the audience contains latent cruelties; the famous Marie Lloyd, like Beckett's Winnie, had perpetually to demean herself, more than any male clown, as a condition of her moral triumph. And *Play*, finally, is School of Ibsen: incomparably the least "realistic" even of Beckett's plays, yet more entangled than any other in mundane tensions (husband, wife, mistress), and more cruelly compliant to the rigors of an audience that will not be appeased until it has known, vicariously, every humiliation these three can inflict on one another. What the audience receives and accepts is of course finely enamelled cliché:

> Judge then of my astoundment when one fine morning, as
> I was sitting stricken in the morning room, he slunk in, fell

on his knees before me, buried his face in my lap and . . . confessed.

This language smoothly parodies itself: "as I was sitting stricken in the morning room." (Does anyone outside of plays ever *speak* the word "stricken"? How does one go about the ritual of "sitting stricken"? Are we to suppose that the morning room is the especially appointed locale for this piece of business?) Yet it is the parody, the fine enamel Beckett applies to his clichés, that makes the doings believable and bearable: we will insist on blood, but we will be satisfied only by formulae.

2

As *Play* moves on from Beckett's earlier plays ("Call that moving," said The Unnamable; "Call that on") so it recapitulates also certain effects developed in the drama for radio. Its three persons (though it is true we can see them) have no names and do nothing but speak, on cue. *Embers* had carried to a seeming limit the major premise of broadcast drama, that it is an affair of voices in a dark world. *Words and Music* pushes this limit back.

MUSIC: *Small orchestra softly tuning up.*
WORDS: Please! (*Tuning. Louder.*) Please! (*Tuning dies away.*) How much longer cooped up here in the dark? (*With loathing.*) With you! (*Pause.*)

These are the opening seconds, and here are the two irreducible conventions of radio, the music and the voice, holding exacerbated dialogue in the dark. Like the bells in *Happy Days*, they have persons attached to them. "Rap of baton on stand" makes it clear that Music is something more than a collective sonorousness, and Words has not only a voice but a set of frayed nerves. Having gotten Music to be quiet, he proceeds to intone an analytic passage on his most congenial passion, which happens to be the anti-passion, Sloth. He is not reciting this either, but composing it, as the missteps and revisions indicate, and we shall later find Music as well engaged in acts of composition.

An imprisoned belletrist, then, and an imprisoned musician, "here in the dark"; they are named, we learn, Joe and Bob; and their master, addressed by no name and designated in the script as "Croak," calls them "my comforts" and implores them, more than once, to be friends. This master can get about; he arrives and leaves on shuffling carpet-slippers; he descends from a tower, plagued on the stairs by the apparition of a face; he calls his "comforts" to order with the thump of a club. All this is eerie melodrama, calmly postulated, as preposterous as the melodrama of the shelter in *Endgame;* are Words and Music perhaps faculties immured in Croak's brain, as Hamm, Clov, Nagg, and Nell occupied a room like the interior of an immense skull? They perform at his bidding, indeed compose in anguish to his bidding, to themes of his announcing. He announces, in succession, three themes: (1) Love, (2) Age ("old age I mean," falters Words, "if that is what my Lord means," and his Lord does not contradict him), and (3) The Face. On Love they expatiate in succession, quarrelling and with little conviction; Words, indeed, simply refurbishes for the occasion his private monologue on Sloth. On Age, with immense reluctance but implacably commanded, they work up a song, revising as they go, feeling their way, Music generally leading; and the horror of Age, this song will have us know is when

> She comes in the ashes
> Who loved could not be won
> Or won not loved...

My Lord's croaking voice next specifies the third theme:

CROAK: (*murmur.*) The face. (*Pause.*) The face. (*Pause.*)
              The face. (*Pause.*) The face.

This, we are to understand, is the face that haunts him on the tower stairs, and detains him and shakes his will; and Words commences to describe how such a face looks when, apparently reclining, it is seen from above, and by starlight.

Seen from above at such close quarters in that radiance so cold and faint with eyes so dimmed by . . . what had passed, its quite . . . piercing beauty is a little . . .

Here some interruptions, after which the voice resumes

. . . blunted. Some moments later, however, such are the powers of recuperation at this age, the head is drawn back to a distance of two or three feet, the eyes widen to a stare and begin to feast again. (*Pause.*) What is then seen would have been better seen in the light of day, that is incontestable.

He proceeds to a frigid inventory of attributes:

—flare of the black disordered hair as though spread wide on water, the brows knitted in a groove suggesting pain but simply concentration more likely all things considered on some consummate inner process, the eyes of course closed in keeping with this, the lashes . . .

It is the familiar Beckett discipline of the specifying phrase and the declarative sentence, bathetic in its pedantry yet heroically right in preferring pedantry to speechless misery. For this is Croak's vanished love, articulated for him by Words in a passage curiously like that reminiscence of passion in a slowly drifting boat which comes back from Krapp's tape again and again ("We lay there without moving. But under us all moved, and moved us, gently, up and down, and from side to side.") Stoically the inventory proceeds downward, hair, brows, eyes, nose, lips, breasts; it is like a Renaissance catalogue of charms, drily paraphrased. Then her face grows suddenly animated, like a reviving Juliet's; "then down a little way. . ."

Here pedantry surrenders; poetry supervenes; and, Music aiding, the language gropes toward a grey epithalamion.

Of course pedantry need not have surrendered, though in this play it did; and it is instructive to examine a refusal of pedantry to surrender, in what reads like the gist of a Science-fiction novel, the thousand-word *Imagination Dead Imagine.* Here an observer, attentive to cycles of light, of temperature, of occulted eyes, scrutinizes amid a lunar whiteness a recumbent couple crammed into a vaulted circle:

Still on the ground, bent in three, the head against the wall at B, the arse against the wall at A, the knees against the wall between B and C, the feet against the wall between C and A, that is to say inscribed in the semicircle ACB, merging in the white ground were it not for the long hair of strangely imperfect whiteness, the white body of a woman finally.

That is his tone, that remains scrupulously his tone, as he examines signs of life ("Hold a mirror to their lips, it mists") or notes "the left eyes which at incalculable intervals suddenly open wide and gaze in unblinking exposure long beyond what is humanly possible . . . Never the two gazes together except once, when the beginning of one overlapped the end of the other, for about ten seconds." They do not gaze into each other's eyes, they lie back to back. And having murmured "ah, no more" and left them, he reflects that there is no other life anywhere and no hope of locating these two again:

> . . . no question now of ever finding again that white speck lost in whiteness, to see if they still lie still in the stress of that storm, or in a worse storm, or in the black dark for good, or the great whiteness unchanging, and if not what they are doing.

So the observer in the story; but Croak in the radio play yields to no such sterility of feeling. He has Words and Music compose him a dismal, gratifying song. To rehearse in the mind, in time of need, the gratifications life never offered, or, offering, saw refused, this is Croak's need and Croak's comfort. It transcends the sexual; it restates Bolton's unspecifiable need for Holloway ("Please! Please!"), and only art or something like art, in this solipsist's nightmare world of dungeons and haunted towers, can make a show of allaying it now. Bolton and Holloway, in the story Henry in *Embers* tells himself, enact repeatedly the need for communion which Henry had denied in his rejection of his wife. Words and Music similarly, though unlike Bolton and Holloway in being faculties rather than puppets, gratify Croak with the ritual articulation of a comparable need. The narrator of *Imagination Dead Imagine* gratifies himself with the chill impossibility of articulating it, of articulating anything but quantifiable fact.

In another radio piece, *Cascando,* a nameless "Opener" also surrenders to need, a Voice and a melodic line again responding. Here things are more austere; there is no hint of Gothic decor, no "Joe" and "Bob," no club, no quarrelling; only the ceremonious "I open," and in response the prompt obedient Voice:

> story . . . if you could finish it . . . you could rest . . . you could sleep . . . not before . . . oh I know . . . the ones I've finished . . . thousands and one . . . all I ever did . . . in my life . . . with my life . . . saying to myself . . . finish this one . . . it's the right one . . . then rest . . .

It is the voice in which Malone, The Unnamable, Hamm, and Henry have told in their time stories to themselves, groping toward repose; it presses on, "low, panting," to limn yet another Beckett vagrant, called Woburn this time; it follows him, as he refuses the hills and presses out to sea; and it is under the unquestionable control of Opener, who can quell it with another ceremonious phrase: "And I close." He can open Music too, and close Music; and he can command Voice and Music to perform in concert, and command them to cease. So with his repertory of openings and closings he directs this strange performance, Voice sketching the shambling tale, Music intervening or sustaining on command, Woburn (in the story) stumbling onto the shingle, collapsing (like the hero of "La Fin") into a boat, committing himself to the waves.

But the air of steely control is an illusion; Opener protests from time to time a suspiciously stoical indifference to what "they" say.

> They say, that is not his life, he does not live on that. They don't see me, they don't see what my life is, they don't see what I live on, and they say, That is not his life, he does not live on that.
> *Pause.*
> I have lived on it . . . pretty long.
> Long enough.
> Listen.

He presses forward with his performance, opening and closing the vocal and instrumental parts, crying as though nearing a climax, "Come on! Come on!" This will be (if he can catch up with Woburn, "see him . . . say him") the last story, that brings peace; and when Voice or Music suddenly flags into silence his consternation is terrible: "Good God good God." He flogs his flagging powers:

> don't let go. . .finish. . .it's the right one. . .I have it. . .this time. . .we're there. . .Woburn. . .nearly—

Yet no more than an act of onanism can the pursuit of Woburn bring communion, and the frenzied music and frenzied words—

> . . .we're there. . .nearly. . .just a few more. . .don't let go . . .Woburn. . .he clings on. . .come on. . .come on—

lapse into a terminal stage direction:

> *Silence.*

In *Film* an implacable hunting-down is prosecuted, subject to no failure of nerve or of resource because conducted by a machine, the camera; conducted therefore on behalf of ourselves, the spectators, who have (have we not?) the *right.* For the camera is our deputy; we look as it looks, moves, pries, pursues, incited by our lust to see the face of a man who does not allow his face to be seen. This man (played by Buster Keaton) "storms along in comic foundered precipitancy," through the street, up the stairs, to his room, followed by a camera (ourselves) which is surprisingly careful to spare him "the anguish of perceivedness": for on two occasions when a glimpse of his face is almost caught it is the camera, not he, that draws back. The camera is less sparing of other faces; once "an elderly couple of shabby genteel aspect" undergoes its scrutiny, and once a frail old flower-woman. The couple is transfixed with horror and hastens away, though its pet monkey is indifferent; apparently "the anguish of perceivedness" is reserved for humans. The flower-woman "closes her eyes, then sinks to the ground and lies with her face in scattered flowers." These people it withers, acutely looking at them, as in the screening-room the Argus-eyed audience acutely looks at them; but until the last implacable confrontation it spares the anonymous "O." (The script calls him O, for Object; the camera is E, for Eye.)

Followed by this intermittently compassionate Eye from the great world (street) through the little world (stairs) to the littlest world (the room), O proceeds to eject or occlude a small universe of Eyes. Window is curtained, mirror covered; dog and cat ("large cat and small dog; unreal quality") are expelled, a ritual requiring seventeen subroutines, each beast repeatedly reentering as he expels the other; the face of God the Father with staring eyes is ripped from the wall and torn in four; the unblinking eye of a parrot and the magnified eye of a goldfish are in turn occulted by an overcoat.

There remains, as for Croak, the past; here a kind of film within the film, as so often in Beckett's work the play within the play or the story within the story; for a film is a blended sequence of stills, and O deals next with seven photographs, his life-story, dealt out one by one as in a time-lapse scrutiny of a flower unfolding. Each features eyes: his mother's "severe eyes devouring" him in infancy, his dog looking up at him, his infant daughter looking into his face, "exploring it with a finger." Only in the seventh picture ("30 years. Looking over 40") is he quite alone; his expression is grim; and his own left eye is covered with a patch. This last picture he destroys, and he then proceeds to destroy each of the others in reverse order, consuming his past as he moves backward through it. (The infant is tough to obliterate; heavier cardboard perhaps.) And now he is alone.

But not alone. The camera waits. It circles him as he sleeps; it fixes his face at last ("patch over left eye") ; its gaze awakens him; they exchange gazes; and finally we are shown *it*. And it has his face. It is ourselves? It is an aspect of himself. "It is O's face (with patch) , but with very different expression, impossible to describe, neither severity nor benignity, but rather acute *intentness*. A big nail is visible near the left temple (patch side) .

Long image of the unblinking gaze." Being a camera, it is mon-ocular and does not blink. Being the suffering O, it bears a nail (it is also a cinematic denizen, so we are not wrong to be remind-ed of Frankenstein's monster). Being intent, it is ourselves. The film is about us, and the selves we go to the cinema to hunt and scrutinize. And it is about the self-scrutiny, the agonizing ulti-mate confrontation no Beckett being can evade. What Krapp confronted listening to his past, what Croak transmuted into commissioned song and Opener into Woburn (though Woburn evades him), what the chill notation of *Imagination Dead Ima-gine* encapsulates into cold fiction and jettisons, O must stare at, we must stare at. "Search of nonbeing in flight from extraneous perception breaking down in inescapability of self perception," runs the script's initial summary of *Film*. And a circle long left open closes; for the final confrontation with the Self occurs in just such a rocking-chair as Murphy, long ago, had taken for the magic cradle of his ritual rock into Nirvana.

In another work another mechanism is equally implacable. The television camera fixes a man named Joe, indeed locks his head into a box in the spectator's living room and holds it there to expand slowly in terror as a toneless voice, a woman's, stabs him with reminiscent phrases. "Thought of everything?" she begins, for he has just closed the window and locked the door and closet, and not omitted to glance under the bed. Is he afraid some bedbug will see him, she asks. It is not bedbugs he fears, as he sits on that bed, but just such memories as her voice brings, and just such self-knowledge: memories that invade the air and fill his motionless head, and are not to be ripped in four as O ripped the photographs. "Eh Joe," she repeats, "Eh Joe . . . Eh Joe . . .," insidiously intimate as he and she were once intimate; and the tale she tells of suicide, of a girl (she says not herself; there have been many girls) who tried with water and knife and finally managed with pills, to be found by the sea with her head pillowed on the stones, perhaps explicates Joe's plight; for he had certainly appreciated this girl, whose post-coital gaze was "unique in his experience," but not appreciated her sufficiently for her not to choose not to live.

3

Work after work rings changes on this inquisitorial theme. At length, in the most extended of these works, *Play* (a title which means that someone or other is playing), the Croak of one radio drama, the Opener of another, the camera of *Film,* the off-camera voice of *Eh Joe,* becomes a spotlight, flicking to and fro across three immobile faces, and soliciting their speech at its whim. It is quite calm, but it will never learn anything new. This light, in a way the chief character, has none of Croak's pathos nor Opener's frenzy; nameless like them, it is voiceless also, more voiceless even than Winnie's minatory bell. It does not participate in the three people's gone passion; no spotlight could. It extracts their story; they are human and other, subject not even to its curiosity but to its mere inquisitorial ritual; and it presses toward no climax but merely toward the moment to begin again, and after that again, having all eternity to play in. The curiosity is wholly ours.

For this is a cunning work, which grants the audience every needful opportunity including the opportunity to hear the whole thing twice. In midcareer it commences to repeat itself exactly[1] and completes the repetition down to the man's terminal question, "Am I as much as . . . being seen?" It then commences a third repetition. We need the recapitulation, as of a film being reshown or a record being replayed, so we can be quite sure what

[1]This account follows the published text throughout. In directing the 1964 London and Paris performances, Beckett virtually improvised a new work (*Play No. 2 ?*) by modifying the rigor of the light. It grew tired; it faded (and the voices with it) ; it relaxed its rigorous sequence for soliciting speeches, so that the second cycle was not identical with the first. Perhaps it would eventually go out and release the players into non-being; or perhaps it was teasing them with this hope. When he prepared the French text for publication (*Comédie,* 1966) , Beckett did not however incorporate these revisions, though he cited them in a note as an alternative mode of performance.

is happening, or what has happened. The play, moreover, needs the recapitulation too, by way of establishing its norm of utterly mechanical recollection in eternal tranquility, as though some cosmic Krapp were intercutting three tapes forever, condemned indeed to intercut them forever, and according to unvarying formulae: for it is very odd that not only do the voices speak the same speeches in the same order, but the spotlight solicits them in the same order too, and accords each fragment of each speech the same duration as the first time, before cutting it off at the same word. Some destiny guides that light, or guides the destiny that guides the light, in a hell of infinite regress. The second half of *Happy Days,* like the second half of *Molloy* or the second half of *Waiting for Godot,* suggests a repetition of the first, though with the slight changes that attend any attempt at repetition in a universe subject to change and entropy. The second half of *Play* is (except for its effect on our minds) identical with the first half of *Play,* in a machine-universe immune from time, change, experience, memory, or communion.

None of the three inhabitants, in this artifice of eternity, knows the other two are there. They are fixed to the chin in huge white urns, "faces so lost to age and aspect as to seem part of the urns." They have each of them a perfectly connected story, recited with interruption but without hiatus; skipping down the printed script, we can read each version through as though the others were not there. Like tapes switched on and off, they seem not to know, until halfway through each cycle, that they are being stopped and started; they merely resume and lapse. They are as nameless as the light that cues them.

Each time round, though, the cycle breaks at mid-point as the three of them, their narratives ended, are overwhelmed by bitter resentment of the flashing light. "Hellish half-light," says the wife. "Get off me! Get off me! . . . Is it that I do not tell the truth, is that it, that some day somehow I may tell the truth at last and then no more light at last, for the truth?" Here is the familiar Beckett ordeal, trying to tell the right story so as to be permitted peace; but each time round she tells the same story, syllable for syllable. The mistress, on the other hand, is tormented by no fierce ideal of truth; she merely supposes (and rather hopes) that the light is driving her out of her wits, and will tire of her when or before it succeeds. Each of them supposes that while she suffers the other lives on, up in the daylight, with the man. As for the man, he knows that he is dead, for he had chosen death. Death is not the peace he had expected, in which "all that pain" would be "as if . . . never been." "It will come. Must come. There is no future in this." He has now revalued, at least, the life in the sun. "I know now, all that was just . . . play. And all this? When will all this—. . . all this, when will all this have been . . . just play?" For the future's role is to reduce the sharp past to "just play": if only it were possible to suppose that ahead of this state lies a future.

What is this state? For him, apparently, death. For them, inquisition, perhaps self-inquisition, whether alive or dead. It is a little as though, after his disappearance, the two women in his life were undergoing a merciless third-degree, whether self-inflicted, or inflicted by officials, or inflicted by the justice that presides over some ante-chamber of hell. They have all three entered, at any rate, the world of *The Unnamable*, or of *How It Is*, where a sunlit life is remembered in fragments; though how people enter this world they never know. They need not know. They are in it. Dante's Belacqua was condemned to dream through again, for as long as he had passed on earth, his life on earth, and Beckett's Murphy, amateur of the "Belacqua bliss," rather cherished the notion of such a post-mortem respite on the threshold of the vigors of heaven. But if life on earth, redreamed, comes to be justly valued as "just play," the act of redreaming it does not. "No doubt I make the same mistake as when it was the sun that shone," says the mistress, "of looking for sense where possibly there is none." And a moment later, "Are you listening to me? Is anyone listening to me? Is anyone looking at me? Is anyone bothering about me at all?"

The audience, of course, is looking and listening; it is the ultimate inquisitor. For Beckett has once again carefully doubled with his play the fact that it is a play, that the actors must repeat it over and over as long as there are spectators who will come, and that those spectators are possessed by a rage to find out: a rage exacerbated by the bizarre surface the author has imparted to this entertainment. The very impediments which his intercutting puts in the way of our finding out what has gone on summon from us an irritated intentness which the work in turn makes use of. *Play* is everything that happens inside the theater, which contains considerably more viewers than actors. And the actors have learned their parts, are letter-perfect in their parts. The viewers have not.

So we strain our attention, and what we find out is soon told. The man was having an affair. His wife accused him, and accused his mistress. Since she had no proof, these accusations had a certain comic edge, not lost on the mistress at least; rage is always tasteless, and the tasteless bizarre. ("What are you talking about, I said, stitching away. Someone yours? Give up whom? I smell you off him, she screamed. He stinks of bitch.") The wife has lost, if she ever had it, whatever sense warns people that they are quoting bad plays. She threatens her own life, threatens the life of the mistress, and even engages a detective. The husband, alarmed by these threats of mayhem, placates each woman by swearing to give up the other. He gives up neither, of course. Eventually he can sustain the double life no longer, and disappears, apparently into death. Perhaps after that the wife carried out her threats; at any rate, they are all three now side by side in the urns.

On earth, they were play-acting, sustained by clichés of language and action. Here is the mistress:

> She came in again. Just strolled in. All honey. Licking her lips. Poor thing. I was doing my nails, by the open window. He has told me all about it, she said. Who he, I said, filing away, and what it? I know what torture you must be going through, she said, and I have come to say I bear you no ill-

feeling. I rung for Arsene.

This is preposterous: the one's compassion, the other's coldness, each speaking in pastiche. Here is the husband:

> At home all heart-to-heart, new leaf and bygones bygones. I ran into your ex-doxy, she said one night, on the pillow, you're well out of that. Rather uncalled-for, I thought. I am indeed, sweetheart, I said, I am indeed. God what vermin women. Thanks to you, angel, I said.

That life was indeed "all play." They assembled its detail out of plays. And now their play, their *jeu des mots,* is indelible. Down in the very rhythm of the sentences, where style assembles well-smoothed epithets compactly, lurks the grotesque falseness which was all any of them could ever really articulate, and which, reciting facts over and over again, they are now condemned to rearticulate forever. That is what they were storing up, all those years, in the famous vessels in which Beckett in *Proust* imagined the finest moments of the past being sealed away: the vessels out of which the voices now come. Theirs is not what the protagonist of "Dante and the Lobster" called ("God help us all") a quick death. There is no quick death, in this Irish post-Protestant world or afterworld. The light too is deathless.

4

An inquisitor, generally not human; and a past to resuffer, transmute, or destroy; permuting these elements through several media Beckett has made this brilliant series of minor works: wrenching, rigorous, ghastly, his great comic gift subsumed into grim precisions of style that render the inquisition ever more refractory. But if we suppose he has boxed himself up we are mistaken, for the little three-minute coda *Come and Go* dispenses with inquisition and obsessive suffering. Its mode is tactful compassion; its agonies, barely touched, perhaps for the future. These woman come and go not in a room but silently, on rubber soles, in and out of a circle of light, and they talk not of Michelangelo but in tactful whispers of another's apparent infirmities. Their age is "undeterminable." Their first words suggest the witches in *Macbeth*: "When did we three last meet?" (The reply is "Let us not speak.") A few lines later they are three little maids from school: "Just sit together as we used to, in the playground at Miss Wade's." Between that time and the present they have undergone the damage of a lifetime, and there may be worse to come; as each in turn leaves briefly, the other two exchange variants of the same dialogue:

FLO: Ru.
RU: Yes.
FLO: What do you think of Vi?
RU: I see little change. (*Flo moves to central seat, whispers in Ru's ear. Appalled.*) Oh! (*They look at each other. Flo puts her finger to her lips.*) Does she not realize?
FLO: God grant not.

Each has this sort of secret to tell of one other; each, having taken part in two such dialogues, perhaps guesses what is being withheld from her, or perhaps does not guess. (How powerful is the argument from analogy? How powerful is willed illusion?) And they hold hands, "Dreaming of . . . love," explicitly not speaking of "the old days" or "of what came after," but thinking they feel on one another's fingers the rings no one can see. Three lives are telescoped into three minutes, in a vignette so spare that each of just 121 spoken words is shaped by dozens of words not spoken. Suffused in their disappointment, sustained by their wistful reenactment, braced by their interlinked connivance to withhold from one another intelligence of rumored agonies, each guilty of having broached the subject on which she must next enjoin reticence, they make of their reticence their lifetime's finest achievement; and Beckett has very nearly made a play out of silence.

Acknowledgments

My information about the country around Foxrock comes from Vivian Mercier; about Alfred Péron, from Ruby Cohn, who also edited the invaluable Beckett issue of *Perspective*; about the theory of irrational numbers, from Tobias Dantzig's *Number, The Language of Science*. An article by Donald Davie in the Winter, 1958 *Spectrum* prompted the stress I have laid on Beckett's syntax, and conversations with the Rev. Walter J. Ong, S.J. my emphasis on the mysteries of voice and person. I am also indebted to four colleagues at the University of California (Santa Barbara) : Donald Pearce, for discussions of *Endgame*, Raymond Federman and John Wilkinson for help with Beckett's French and Geulincx's Latin, Alan Stephens for his critical reading of the finished typescript. Translations from Beckett's French works are his own with the following exceptions: *Molloy* was translated by Patrick Bowles and the *Nouvelles* ("The End" and "L'Expulsé") by Richard Seaver, both in collaboration with the author. All other translations are my own.

Earlier versions of portions of this book have appeared in *Spectrum, Forum, National Review,* and *Perspective,* to the editors of which I am indebted for permission to revise and reprint.

The last chapter, "Progress Report," is based on an essay I wrote for the Festschrift *Beckett at Sixty,* published by Calder and Boyars (London 1967) , and is used here by the kind permission of Calder and Boyars Ltd. The essay in turn is adapted from a supplementary chapter I wrote in 1964 for the German translation of the present book, published in Munich by Carl Hanser Verlag.